The War of 1812

The War of 1812

A Short History

Bicentennial Edition

DONALD R. HICKEY

University of Illinois Press

URBANA, CHICAGO, AND SPRINGFIELD

∞ This book is printed on acid-free paper.

Library of Congress Cataloging-in-Publication Data
Hickey, Donald R., 1944–
The War of 1812 : a short history / Donald R. Hickey.—Bicentennial ed.
        p.   cm.
Includes bibliographical references and index.
ISBN 978-0-252-07877-4 (pbk. : acid-free paper)—ISBN 978-0-252-09447-7 (e-book)
1. United States—History—War of 1812. I. Title.
           E354.H535   2012
     973.5'2—dc23   2012013874

Contents

Preface to Bicentennial Edition   vii

Preface to First Edition   ix

Introduction   1

1. The Coming of the War, 1801–1812   5

2. The Campaign of 1812   19

3. The Campaign of 1813   40

4. The British Counteroffensive, 1814–1815   60

5. The Inner War   87

6. The Peace of Christmas Eve   103

Legacies   115

Chronology   123

Suggestions for Further Reading   133

Index   135

Preface to Bicentennial Edition

In the mid-1980s, I decided to write a short book on the War of 1812 that would be suitable for college-level U.S. history survey courses, but the project soon took on a life of its own. The result was a full-blown military, political, and diplomatic history of the war that was published in 1989 as *The War of 1812: A Forgotten Conflict.* Several years later, I decided to put out an abridged version of this book that I hoped would serve my original purpose. The result was *The War of 1812: A Short History,* which was published in 1995.

I recently put out a new edition of *A Forgotten Conflict* to correct errors and incorporate new material from the many works that had appeared, particularly on the war's military history, since the first edition was published. The same logic suggested that I revise *A Short History.*

I have rewritten virtually every chapter although the most significant changes are in the three military chapters. I have also included new material on the legacy of the war, which has been little studied by scholars and yet seems to me to warrant serious consideration.

I have tried to make this work easier to read by including subheadings. I have also added illustrations and a new set of maps, and I've revised the Chronology and the Suggestions for Further Reading. Although the University of Illinois Press had provided me with an electronic copy of the original work, I produced this manuscript from scratch. I kept the original book before me, but I undoubtedly made more changes than if I were just tweaking the electronic copy. The new edition is a little over 50,000 words, about 25 percent longer than the original version. Although this work is essentially an abridgement of the revised edition of *A Forgotten Conflict,* I have made a few corrections and added some fresh material. The sources for all quotations can be found in the longer work.

Preface to First Edition

This book is a condensed version of my study, *The War of 1812: A Forgotten Conflict*, which was published by the University of Illinois Press in 1989. That work enjoyed a fairly wide audience, mainly through the Book-of-the-Month Club and the History Book Club. My aim here is to present the essentials of that study in abbreviated form. The original work was 118,000 words and included 115 pages of notes. I have dropped the notes and trimmed the text by almost two-thirds—to about 40,000 words. Most of the cuts were made in the domestic history although I also compressed the diplomatic history and eliminated some details from the military and naval campaigns. I have modernized the capitalization, spelling, and punctuation of all contemporary quotations. I have also added a chronology. As in the original study, the maps have been put at the end of the text to facilitate use.

For helpful criticism of an early draft of this work, I am indebted to Vance Burke, Connie Clarke, and Bob McColley.

The War of 1812

Introduction

The War of 1812 is probably our most obscure major war. It lacks the grand scope and significance of the Revolution, the Civil War, and the world wars, and it is buried too deep in the past to compete in the public memory with the wars in Korea or Vietnam or our more recent conflicts in Iraq and Afghanistan. The Indian wars in the nineteenth century are better known, and the same may also be true for our wars of domestic and overseas expansion—the Mexican War (1846–1848) and the Spanish-American War (1898).

The average American is only vaguely aware of who our enemy was in the War of 1812 or why we fought. Even those who know something about the conflict are likely to remember only a few of the more dramatic highlights, such as the burning of the nation's capital, the defense of Fort McHenry and the writing of the national anthem, and Andrew Jackson's spectacular victory at New Orleans.

Why is this war so obscure? One reason is that no great president is associated with the contest. Although his Federalist enemies called it "Mr. Madison's War," President James Madison was not a strong leader and thus never put his stamp on the conflict. In addition, the fighting was too diffuse to enable any one general to lead the nation to victory. In the land war, there were seven theaters of operation—four on the Canadian-American border, a fifth in the Chesapeake, a sixth in the Southwest, and a seventh on the Gulf Coast—and arguably the high seas constituted an eighth theater of operations. The war produced a number of successful army leaders—William Henry Harrison on the Detroit frontier, Jacob Brown and Winfield Scott on the Niagara frontier, and Andrew Jackson in the Southwest and on the Gulf Coast—but given the scope of the conflict, it was impossible for any of these men to shape the broader outcome of the war. There was no one like George Washington, Ulysses Grant, or Dwight Eisenhower that we can credit with leading the nation to victory.

Another reason for the obscurity of this war is that the causes are complex and still subject to debate. It is often difficult to nail down the causes of a war because (especially in a democracy) many people may have a role in the decision and each may support war for a different reason. Even when one person plays a central role in the decision-making, he might have multiple and even contradictory reasons for favoring war.

Most scholars today agree that the United States went to war in 1812 mainly over maritime issues. The principal U.S. aim was to force the British to give up the Orders-in-Council, which restricted American trade with the European Continent, and impressment, which was the Royal Navy's practice of removing seamen from American merchant ships to fill out the crews of its warships. According to this school of thought, war in 1812 was undertaken (in the language of the day) to uphold "Free Trade and Sailors' Rights."

There are, however, other schools of thought. Some writers have insisted that the nation's real aim was to seize Canada in order to put an end to British influence over American Indians or to secure additional farmland. Others have focused on ideological factors—the desire to preserve American honor, uphold national prestige, and demonstrate that the fragile young Republic could defend its rights in a war-torn world. There is even a school of thought that has emphasized the political origins of the war, that is, the determination of the Jeffersonian Republicans to use war as a vehicle to forge party unity, preserve national power, and silence their Federalist critics. It is possible, even likely, that all of these issues played some role in causing the war, although scholars have reached no consensus on their relative importance.

If the causes of the war are subject to debate, so, too, is the outcome. The United States has won most of its wars, often securing significant concessions from a defeated foe, but the War of 1812 was different. Far from bringing the enemy to terms, the United States was lucky to escape without making extensive concessions itself. In fact, none of the issues that caused the war were mentioned in the peace treaty. What does this suggest about the outcome of the war? Was it, as many contemporaries claimed, an American victory, or is it more accurately judged a draw or perhaps even a defeat? On these matters, scholars have been unable to agree.

One issue that scholars have agreed on is that the conduct of the war was marked by considerable bungling and mismanagement. This was partly due to the nature of the Republic. The new nation was simply too young and immature, and its government too feeble and inexperienced, to prosecute a major war efficiently. Politics also played a role. Federalists vigorously opposed the war, and so, too, did some Republicans. Even those who supported the war feuded among themselves and never displayed the sort of patriotic enthusiasm that has characterized other American wars. The advocates of war appeared to support the conflict more with their heads than their hearts, and more with their hearts than their purses. As a result, efforts to recruit enough men to wage successful campaigns and to raise enough money to pay for them lagged consistently behind need.

Despite all the bungling and halfhearted support, the War of 1812 was not without its stirring moments and splendid victories. The U.S. triumph at the Thames in the Old Northwest, the rousing defense of Baltimore, and Jackson's epic victory at New Orleans—all of these showed that with the right leadership, training, and equipment, the American fighting man could hold his own against the disciplined and battle-hardened regulars of Great Britain. In addition, the American naval victories on the northern lakes and the high seas vindicated the nation's rich maritime tradition and showed that even the mighty Mistress of the Seas could not take victory for granted against what one British cabinet official called "these second-hand Englishmen."

The war also produced its share of heroes, people whose reputation was enhanced by wartime service in the government or in the field. The war helped catapult four men into the presidency—James Monroe, John Quincy Adams, Andrew Jackson, and William Henry Harrison—and three men into the vice presidency—Daniel D. Tompkins, John C. Calhoun, and Richard M. Johnson. The war gave a significant boost to the political or military careers of a host of other young men, most notably Henry Clay in Congress, Jacob Brown and Winfield Scott in the army, and Oliver H. Perry and Thomas Macdonough in the navy. Indeed, for many ambitious young men, the war offered an excellent launching pad for a career.

In some ways, the War of 1812 looked more to the past than to the future. As the second and last war that the United States fought against Great Britain, it echoed the ideology and issues of the American Revolution. Indeed, Republicans commonly called it a "second war of independence." It was also the second and last time that the United States was the underdog in a war and the second and last time that the nation tried to conquer Canada. This war stands apart from other early American wars in generating such adamant political opposition and in ending without a clear-cut victory. Although most Americans pretended that they had won the war, they were hard-pressed to identify any concrete gains.

It is this lack of clear-cut success that may best explain why the war is so little remembered today. Americans have characteristically judged their wars on the basis of their success. The best known wars—the Revolution, the Civil War, and World War II—were all spectacular successes that marked important benchmarks in the Republic's history. The War of 1812, by contrast, does not fit this template. It lacks the kind of clear and compelling accomplishments that are plain to anyone who studies the war. And this may be why the war attracts so little interest or attention today.

But appearances can be deceptive, and the obscurity of this war should not blind us to its significance. It may not be obvious to the casual observer, but the War of 1812 was an important turning point, a great watershed that shaped the political, military, and diplomatic future of the young Republic. It concluded almost a quarter century of partisan politics and troubled diplomacy and ushered in the Era of Good

Feelings and a period of sustained and prosperous isolationism. It marked the end of the Federalist party but the vindication of Federalist policies, many of which were adopted by the Republicans during or after the war. It broke the power of American Indians in both the Old Northwest and the Old Southwest and left them without any allies in America, thus tipping the balance of power on the continent decisively against them. It also reinforced the powerful undercurrent of Anglophobia that had been present since the American Revolution and that would not finally dissipate until the twentieth century. More broadly, the war produced the national self-confidence and supercharged the heady expansionism that lay at the heart of American foreign policy for the rest of the century.

Above all, the war transformed the cultural landscape of the new nation. It gave Americans a host of symbols and sayings—"Old Ironsides" and the Kentucky rifle, the Fort McHenry flag and the national anthem, "Don't give up the ship" and "We have met the enemy and they are ours"—that helped Americans define who they were and where they were headed. Although looking to the past, the war was fraught with consequences for the future, and for this reason it is worth studying today.

Chapter 1

The Coming of the War, 1801–1812

On March 4, 1801, Thomas Jefferson walked from his boardinghouse in Washington City, as the nation's new capital was then called, to the Capitol Building, where he was inaugurated as third president of the United States. The ceremony was short and Spartan. The nation's new leaders favored a simpler and more democratic style than their Federalist predecessors. They also planned to adopt a new set of policies. It was these policies—initiated by Jefferson and carried on by his friend and successor, James Madison—that put the United States on a collision course with Great Britain and ultimately led to the War of 1812.

Republicans did not differ with Federalists over the broad objectives of American policy in this era. The French Revolution, which had erupted in 1789, plunged Europe into warfare. Known as the French Revolutionary and Napoleonic Wars, this conflict lasted from 1792 to 1815. Essentially a world war, the struggle cast a long shadow across the Atlantic as the two leading belligerents, Great Britain and France, repeatedly encroached on American rights in the pursuit of victory. During this era of sustained warfare, all Americans agreed that the new nation should promote prosperity at home while protecting its rights and preserving its neutrality abroad. But what was the best way to achieve these ends? It was this question, more than any other, that divided Americans into two political camps.

The Federalist Ascendancy (1789–1801)

The Federalists, who controlled the national government in the 1790s, subscribed to the old Roman doctrine that the best way to avoid war was to prepare for it. Under the leadership of President George Washington and Secretary of the Treasury Alexander Hamilton, they implemented a broad program of financial and military preparedness. Besides adopting Hamilton's financial program (which included trade and excise taxes, a funded national debt, and a national bank), they expanded the army, built a navy, and launched a rudimentary system of coastal fortifications. Their aim was not simply to deter war but to put the nation in a position to fight and finance a war if hostilities ever erupted.

Besides embracing preparedness at home, the Federalists pursued a pro-British foreign policy abroad. The cornerstone of this policy was the Jay Treaty, an Anglo-American agreement negotiated in 1794 that regulated commerce between the two nations and defined Britain's belligerent rights and America's neutral rights in the European war. The Republicans, who never got over their fear and hatred of Britain from the American Revolution, denounced the Jay Treaty as a one-sided sellout of American interests. In a typical Republican editorial, one newspaper called it the "death-warrant to our neutral rights." Whatever its liabilities, there is no denying that the Jay Treaty served American interests in two important ways. It ensured peace with the Mistress of the Seas, the one nation that could seriously threaten the young Republic's growing trade. It also ushered in an era of friendship with Britain that allowed American trade, and hence the entire American economy, to flourish. American exports, which stood at $33 million in 1794, nearly tripled to $94 million in 1801.

The only liability of the Jay Agreement was that it infuriated France, which was still nominally bound to the United States by a treaty of alliance the two nations had signed in 1778 during the American Revolution. Determined to bully the United States into repudiating the Jay Treaty, France severed diplomatic ties and unleashed its warships and privateers on American trade. This led to the Quasi-War, an undeclared naval war with France that lasted from 1798 to 1801. The new Federalist navy acquitted itself well in this war. Cruising mainly in the Caribbean, where most of the French depredations had occurred, the navy defeated or destroyed three French warships (while losing only one of its own), captured eighty-two French privateers, and recovered seventy American merchant vessels that were in French hands. In response to U.S. determination, France called off its war on American trade and agreed to restore normal relations.

Although their policies in the 1790s had served the nation reasonably well, the Federalists were voted out of office in 1800. Their approach to politics was too elitist for the rising spirit of democracy in this era and their pro-British foreign policy ran counter to the widespread distrust and hatred of Britain that was a legacy of the American Revolution. In addition, some of their policies during the Quasi-War—a boost in taxation and the adoption of the repressive alien and sedition laws—were unpopular with many Americans. As a result, the Republicans won control of the presidency and both houses of Congress.

The Republicans Take Control (1801)

When the Republicans took office in 1801, they reversed many of the policies that they had inherited from the Federalists. Convinced that the excise taxes discriminated against their constituents in the South and West, they repealed these duties in 1802, and regarding the national bank as an aristocratic monopoly subject to foreign control, they refused to renew its charter when it expired in 1811. Preferring to rely on militia and privateers as well as small and inexpensive gunboats, the Republicans trimmed the army and took most of the navy's warships out of service. They also used the army's officer corps as a dumping ground for the party faithful.

Although these policies weakened the nation financially and militarily, they were popular with the American people and initially at least did no harm. Great Britain and France concluded the preliminary Peace of Amiens in 1801 and remained at peace until 1803. When the European war resumed, both belligerents once again interfered with American trade and encroached on American rights. Because the British controlled

James Madison (1751–1836) was president during the War of 1812. He was not a strong leader and was unable to impose his will on Congress or to inspire the country. (J. A. Spencer, *History of the United States*)

the high seas, most Americans found their behavior more offensive. Soon a whole range of issues emerged to drive the two English-speaking nations apart.

Impressment and the Orders-in-Council

To fill out the crews of its chronically undermanned warships, the Royal Navy routinely stopped American merchant ships on the high seas and impressed or drafted seamen into service. Although the press gangs were supposed to target only British seamen, through accident or design a fair number of American citizens got caught in the dragnet. Between 1803 and 1812, an estimated 6,000 American tars (as seamen were then called) were forced to serve on British warships.

British officials were willing to release any Americans whose citizenship could be proven, but this could only be done through diplomatic channels, a process that could take years. In the meantime, American victims of impressment were subjected to all the misery of British naval service (where discipline was enforced with the cat-o'-nine tails) and to all the horrors of a war that was not their own. Moreover, any impressed tar who accepted the enlistment bounty while in service was considered a volunteer regardless of any evidence of citizenship that might be produced.

Besides impressing seamen from American ships, the British periodically interfered with America's lucrative trade with the West Indies and often violated American territorial waters, conducting searches and making seizures within the three-mile limit. In addition, they made sweeping use of naval blockades to close off the trade of their enemies, and they insisted on a much broader definition of contraband than the United States was willing to concede.

The British offered to resolve some of these problems in the Monroe–Pinkney Treaty of 1806. This agreement was designed as a successor to the Jay Treaty (most of whose clauses had expired in 1803), although in the realm of commerce and neutral rights it was actually more favorable to the United States. But President Jefferson found it so unsatisfactory (mainly because it did not address the issue of impressment) that he refused to submit it to the Senate for approval. The loss of this treaty was a great turning point in the period. By rejecting the agreement, the United States missed a chance to re-forge the Anglo-American accord of the 1790s and to take a road that might have led to peace and prosperity instead of one that led to trade restrictions and war.

After the loss of the Monroe–Pinkney Treaty, Anglo-American relations steadily deteriorated. In the summer of 1807 there was a full-blown war scare when the British frigate *Leonard* (52 guns) fired on the U.S. frigate *Chesapeake* (40 guns), killing and wounding a number of the crew. After the *Chesapeake* surrendered, the British removed four seamen that were deserters from the Royal Navy. The British government did not claim the right to search or impress from neutral warships (which were considered an extension of a nation's territory), and it disavowed the attack and offered to pay compensation. But the issue became entangled with others, and a settlement was delayed until 1811. In the meantime, the *Chesapeake* affair festered, contributing to the rising tide of anti-British feeling in the United States and the drift toward war.

Shortly after the *Chesapeake* outrage, another problem surfaced that was to bedevil Anglo-American relations even more. This was the Orders-in-Council, a series of executive decrees issued by the British government between 1807 and 1809 that sharply curtailed American trade with the European Continent. The British conceded that the Orders did not accord with international law but justified them as a necessary response to Napoleon's Continental Decrees, which prohibited all trade with the British Isles. This did little to pacify Americans, who believed, with some justice, that both belligerents were using their anti-commercial war as a pretext to loot American trade. American losses were considerable. Between 1807 and 1812, Great Britain and France and their allies seized some 900 American ships.

The Restrictive System (1806–1811)

To combat the growing assault on American commerce, Republicans adopted their own restrictions on trade. Known collectively as the restrictive system, these measures grew out of the Republican belief that American trade could be used as an instrument of foreign policy. The underlying assumption was that Great Britain (and to a lesser degree France) and their West Indian colonies needed the United States as a source for food and other raw materials and as a market for their finished projects. By limiting or cutting off American trade, the Republicans believed they could force the European belligerents to show greater respect for the young Republic's neutral rights.

In 1806 Congress enacted a partial non-importation act that prohibited a select list of British imports. In 1807 Congress added a general embargo that prohibited all American exports. In 1809 these measures were repealed in favor of a non-intercourse act that permitted trade with the rest of the world but barred all trade with Britain, France, and their colonies. This law was repealed in 1810, but in 1811 Congress passed a fresh non-importation law that prohibited all imports from Britain.

These measures failed to win any concessions from the belligerents but instead boomeranged on the United States, destroying American prosperity and depriving the federal government of much-needed revenue that normally came from taxes on trade. American exports fell from a peak of $108 million in 1807 to a low of $22 million in 1808, and American imports declined from a high of $139 million in 1807 to a low of $53 million in 1811. In a similar vein, government revenue, which peaked at $17 million in 1808, fell to less than $8 million in 1809. The ineffectiveness of the restrictive system exposed Republicans to sharp criticism from the Federalists, who had opposed Republican foreign policy ever since the loss of the Monroe–Pinkney Treaty.

Growing Tension (1811)

Two other developments contributed to the deterioration of Anglo-American relations in 1811. The first was the *Little Belt* incident, a kind of *Chesapeake* affair in reverse, in which the U.S. frigate *President* (54 guns) exchanged fire at night with the much smaller British sloop *Little Belt* (20 guns), killing and wounding a number of the crew. Since it was never clear who fired first, the British chose not to make an issue of the matter, although many Americans considered it just retaliation for the *Chesapeake* affair.

The other development was the outbreak of an Indian war in the Old Northwest. This conflict was an outgrowth of a series of dubious land cession treaties that William Henry Harrison, governor of the Indiana Territory, had imposed on the Indians, culminating in the Treaty of Fort Wayne in 1809. This treaty was the last straw for two Shawnee brothers, Tecumseh and Tenskwatawa (better known as the Prophet), who headed an Indian confederation opposed to the further loss of Indian lands and the destruction of the traditional native way of life.

Harrison's policies led to a growing number of Indian raids on the frontier. Because the Indians got the bulk of their supplies (including their muskets) from the

This contemporary cartoon suggests that the British were behind Indian raids on the American frontier before the War of 1812. In truth, the British sought to restrain their native allies but were not always successful. (Watercolor etching by William Charles. Library of Congress)

British in Canada, most Americans were convinced that the British were behind the raids. "We have had but one opinion as [to] the cause of the depredations of the Indians," said *Niles' Register.* "They are instigated and supported by the British in Canada."

In the fall of 1811 Harrison marched into Indian territory to break up the native settlement at Prophetstown, which was on the Wabash River just below the mouth of the Tippecanoe River. The result was the Battle of Tippecanoe on November 7. Although Harrison suffered heavy casualties, he drove off the Indians and then burned their village and food supplies. This marked the beginning of an Indian war that later blended into the War of 1812. The outbreak of the Indian war rendered the entire frontier unsafe. "Most of the citizens in this country," Harrison reported in 1812, "have abandoned their farms and taken refuge in such temporary forts as they have been able to construct."

The War Congress Meets

By the time the Twelfth Congress—known to history as the War Congress—met on November 4, 1811, there was growing talk of the war. The British had made no concessions on the issues in dispute, and any settlement of the leading issues—the Orders-in-Council and impressment—seemed remote. Many Republicans were frustrated with the restrictive system, which seemed to do more harm to the United States than to Britain or France. To a growing number of Republicans, war seemed to be the only answer.

The Republicans had solid majorities in both houses of Congress, controlling 75 percent of the seats in the House and 82 percent in the Senate. But for years the party had lacked competent floor leadership and been torn apart by factionalism. The regular Republicans, who usually followed the administration's lead, could usually muster a majority, but on occasion dissident members of the party combined with Federalists to block legislation. "Factions in our party," complained one Republican, "have hitherto been the bane of the Democratic administration."

Fortunately for the administration, there was a new faction in the War Congress capable of providing the leadership and firmness that hitherto had been lacking. These were the War Hawks, a group of about a dozen ardent patriots who came mainly from the South and West. Too young to remember the horrors of the last British war, the War Hawks were willing to hazard another contest to vindicate the nation's rights.

Heading the War Hawks was young Henry Clay of Kentucky. Although not yet thirty-five and never before a member of the House, Clay was elected speaker and lost no time in establishing his authority. Heretofore, the speakership had been largely ceremonial, but Clay molded the office into a position of power, and, as one contemporary put it, he "reduced the chaos to order." By directing debate and interpreting the rules, by packing key committees with War Hawks and by acting forcefully behind the scenes, Clay kept the war movement on track.

War Preparations (1811–1812)

The president submitted his opening address to Congress on November 5, 1811. Focusing on the Orders-in-Council, Madison accused Great Britain of making "war on our lawful commerce" and urged Congress to put the nation "into an armor and an attitude demanded by the crisis." Congress responded by adopting a comprehensive program of war preparations. The army was expanded, the recruitment of short-term volunteers was authorized, and the militia was readied for service. The nation's warships were put into service, and money was appropriated to purchase munitions and other war material and to build and repair coastal fortifications. A war loan was also authorized, although Republicans refused to consider new taxes until war was actually declared.

Most of the war preparations were adopted by large majorities, but the voting masked deep-seated differences. The War Hawks supported these measures as a prelude to war, and Republicans from commercial districts because they had long advocated stronger defense measures, especially for the protection of the nation's trade. But there were some Republicans—the "scarecrow party"—who supported the war program in the hope that the mere threat of war would frighten the British into concessions.

Republicans were also divided on how best to wage war. Although all agreed that Canada should be targeted, they could not agree whether the job could best be done by long-term regulars, short-term volunteers, or militia. Nor could they agree on whether the navy ought to be expanded to challenge the British on the high seas. Most divisive of all was the tax issue since any new taxes were sure to be unpopular and might undermine support for the war.

The Federalists offered little resistance to the war measures and even supported some of them. They were eager to avoid the charge that they were pawns of Great Britain, and they had long favored military and naval preparedness. They were particularly interested in naval expansion, believing that the best place to defend the nation's trade and neutral rights was on the high seas. "If you had a field to defend in Georgia," said Congressman Josiah Quincy of Massachusetts, "it would be very strange to put up a fence in Massachusetts. And yet, how does this differ from invading Canada for the purpose of defending our maritime rights?" Most Republicans, however, preferred to focus on Canada, and proposals to increase the navy went down to defeat.

The War Hawks hoped that their program would prepare the nation militarily and psychologically for war. President Madison hoped for the same result, and he used the powers of his office to stimulate the war spirit. On March 9, 1812, as the

War Hawks were putting the final touches on their war program, the president informed Congress of a British plot to incite disunion in Federalist New England. To support this accusation, Madison submitted documents from a British spy named John Henry, who had visited New England in 1808–1809.

Republicans expressed outrage at the Henry affair, and the semi-official Washington *National Intelligencer* expressed hope that Henry's papers would "become a bond of union against a common foe." But their effect was just the opposite. A close examination of the documents revealed that Henry had implicated no one but had simply reported to British officials on political conditions in New England. Federalists were furious over this attempt to impugn their loyalty. Moreover, by tracing the Treasury warrants that were used to pay Henry, the Federalists learned that the documents had been purchased for the princely sum of $50,000—rather than freely given, as Henry's cover letter had implied. This only added to the Federalists' outrage and to the embarrassment of Republicans.

Public Expectations

In early April, just as the dust raised by the Henry affair was settling, Congress took another step toward war by enacting a ninety-day embargo and a ninety-day non-exportation law. These measures prohibited American ships from clearing for foreign ports and barred the export of all goods and money by land or by sea. The War Hawks promoted this legislation as a forerunner to war. If the American sloop *Hornet*, which was expected from Europe shortly, did not bring news of British concessions, the War Hawks were determined to push ahead with war.

Although the War Hawks insisted that the purpose on the new trade legislation was to protect American property by keeping ships and cargoes in port, the public did not believe that war was imminent. News of the two laws led to a flurry of activity along the seaboard as merchants rushed to get their ships to sea before the ports could be closed. Freight rates jumped 20 percent, and many vessels were loaded and sent to sea in just two days. Republicans no less than Federalists took part in the frenzy of activity. "In this *hurly-burly* to palsy the arm of the government," conceded *Niles' Register*, "justice compels us to say that all parties united."

The rush to get ships to sea made a mockery of the entire war movement. "The great body of people," said *Niles' Register*, "have acted as though an adjustment of differences with Great Britain, instead of an appeal to the sword, was at hand." Shipping insurance—a good indication of public expectations—remained low in early 1812, even for ships sailing to Great Britain. "We hear from all quarters," commented a War Hawk in late March, "that the people do not expect war."

Federalists were particularly skeptical of the war talk. In a highly publicized speech delivered in 1809, Josiah Quincy had claimed that the Republican majority "could not be kicked into war." Nothing in the years that followed altered Quincy's opinion. Even after the War Congress had assembled, Quincy claimed that the talk of war was "ludicrous" and that even "the highest toned of the war party" conceded privately that hostilities were unlikely. Most Federalists shared this view, believing that Republicans would ultimately opt for more trade restrictions.

The government was partly responsible for this skepticism. Talk of war in the past had never led to hostilities, and the administration continued to send out mixed signals. As late as March 31, Secretary of State James Monroe sounded very much like a member of the scarecrow party when he told a House committee that the war preparations were designed mainly to *"appeal to the feelings of the [British] government."* The administration also kept Augustus J. Foster, the British minister in Washington, in the dark. By early May Foster was so confused that he told a British consul that "so absolutely are they here without chart or compass that I really am at a loss to give you news."

Republicans in Congress were also sending mixed signals. "The war fever," reported a House Federalist, "has its hot and cold fits." It was well known that some Republicans had voted for the ninety-day embargo as a coercive instrument (in line with the restrictive system), which undermined the War Hawks' claim that it was a preliminary to war. Moreover, many members were so weary from the long session that there was considerable interest in a recess that one Republican claimed would "damp the public spirit and paralyze the energies of the nation." Although several proposals for a recess were voted down, many congressmen went home anyway.

A Baltimore newspaper circulated a rumor that a special diplomatic mission would be sent to Great Britain to avert war. The report, which was widely credited and was repeated as far away as London, said that to preserve peace the British had offered to resurrect the Monroe–Pinkney Treaty, with modifications favorable to the United States. With rumors like this afloat, it is hardly surprising that so many people remained skeptical about the prospects for war.

British Concessions

Great Britain, like the United States, was also sending mixed signals, but it was heading in the opposite direction, hoping through a series of conciliatory gestures to avert war. The first step was the settlement of the *Chesapeake* affair in late 1811. After more than four years of sparring, the two powers finally managed to divorce this issue from others and reach a settlement. The problem had festered for so long, however, that most Americans found little satisfaction in the resolution. Returning the impressed seamen, said the Baltimore *Whig*, was "like restoring a hair after fracturing the skull."

In the spring of 1812, the Royal Navy began to treat American ships and seamen with new tact. The Admiralty ordered all naval officers to take "especial care" to avoid clashes with the U.S. Navy and to exercise "all possible forbearance" toward American citizens. The commanding officers at both Halifax and Bermuda ordered their ships to keep clear of the American coast to avoid incidents. This was particularly important because Americans found British searches and seizures near the coast so galling.

In May 1812, on the very eve of war, the British offered to give the United States an equal share of their trade with the European continent, which was conducted under special licenses. Inasmuch as the British had issued an average of ten thousand licenses a year since 1807, this proposal was significant. In effect, the British were offering to suspend the Orders-in-Council in practice if American merchants would conduct their trade with Europe under British licenses. Believing that accepting the British proposal would be tantamount to surrendering U.S. independence, the administration summarily rejected it.

The British made their greatest concession the following month just as the United States was declaring war. On June 16—two days before the declaration of war— Lord Castlereagh announced in Parliament that the Orders-in-Council would be withdrawn if the United States suspended the last major prewar trade restriction, the non-importation law of 1811. A week later, without waiting for the American response, the ministry scrapped the whole system of blockades and licenses, thus eliminating the principal cause of war. Had there been a transatlantic cable, this news might have averted war. But without a speedy means of communication, the news did not reach Washington until August 13, and by then it was too late.

The President Recommends War

Although the Republicans did not realize that the British were making concessions, they hoped that the return of the *Hornet* would bring news of a new policy. The long overdue ship finally arrived in New York on May 19, and the dispatches it carried reached Washington three days later. The news, however, was doubly disappointing. Although unofficial reports suggested a softening of British policy, official statements indicated a stubborn adherence to the Orders-in-Council. The news from France was no better, for despite a promise to rescind the Continental Decrees, the French continued to loot American commerce. For Americans hoping for concessions from at least one of the belligerents, the news from Europe was disappointing indeed.

The War Hawks had long before agreed that if the *Hornet* arrived without news of British concessions, they would push for war. Although the Constitution entrusted this decision to Congress, the War Hawks wanted the president to take the lead. Madison did not disappoint them. On June 1, less than ten days after the *Hornet's* dispatches arrived, he sent a secret message to Congress on the subject of Anglo-American relations.

Madison's message was a powerful indictment of Great Britain. The British were arraigned for impressing American seamen; violating U.S. waters; establishing illegal blockades, particularly "the sweeping system of blockades under the name of

Orders-in-Council"; sending a secret agent (John Henry) to subvert the Union; and exerting a malicious influence over the Indians in the Old Northwest. The message emphasized maritime issues. Fully two-thirds of the document was devoted to the Orders-in-Council and other naval blockades.

Madison's message was uncharacteristically angry and in places echoed the Declaration of Independence, reflecting the Republican view that a second war of independence was needed to put an end to Britain's quasi-colonial practices of regulating American trade and impressing American seamen. Because the decision for war rested with Congress, Madison did not actually make a recommendation, but the thrust of his message was clear. "We behold . . . on the side of Great Britain," he said, "a state of war against the United States; and on the side of the United States a state of peace towards Britain."

Congress Declares War

In the House of Representatives, Madison's message was referred to the Foreign Relations Committee, which issued a report sharply critical of Britain, especially for the Orders-in-Council. Shortly thereafter, John C. Calhoun, a War Hawk from South Carolina, introduced a bill declaring war. When the Republicans refused to come out of secret session to debate the measure, Federalists decided to remain silent. As a result, Republicans were able to push the bill through the House in only two days, a remarkably short time for so important a measure. The final vote on the war bill was seventy-nine to forty-nine.

In the Senate the bill ran into more trouble. There was considerable support in the Senate for limiting the war to the high seas. This appealed to many people because it offered a direct means of vindicating the nation's rights at sea and was likely to be cheaper than an extended land war. The main problem with this strategy was that the British were far more vulnerable in sparsely populated Canada than on the high seas. The U.S. Navy was no match for the Royal Navy, and even if American privateers covered the ocean they might not do enough damage to bring the British to terms.

Although some Republicans (including Monroe and other members of the cabinet) favored a limited maritime war, the Federalists were the most vocal proponents of this strategy. Doubtless recalling the success of the Quasi-War against France in 1798, the Federalists for years had been calling for expanding the navy and arming merchantmen. Most agreed with Josiah Quincy that the nation had a duty to provide "systematic protection of our maritime rights by maritime means."

No doubt some Federalists supported maritime war simply as the lesser of two evils—maybe not desirable in itself but preferable to full-scale war. Yet for most, a war restricted to the high seas offered the best means of upholding the nation's rights, especially if (as was widely assumed) France was included in the reprisals.

This would enable Federalist merchants to choose the enemy. Unleashing armed merchantmen against both European belligerents, said a Federalist newspaper in a widely reprinted editorial, "meets our peculiar approbation."

The Senate referred the House's war bill to a select committee, which reported it with little change on June 8. The following day, however, Republican Andrew Gregg of Pennsylvania moved to send the bill back to committee with instructions to amend it so that it merely gave the president authority to unleash American warships and privateers on Britain. Gregg's motion carried, seventeen to thirteen. Three days later, however, when the modified bill was reported from committee, the Senate reversed itself. A motion to accept the committee's changes failed by a tie vote, sixteen to sixteen, when president pro tem John Gaillard of South Carolina cast his vote against it. The tie vote meant that the original bill was restored.

Although proponents of full-scale war prevailed, the outcome was long in doubt. It took the Senate two weeks to complete its deliberations on the war bill, which prompted one House Republican to exclaim: "The suspense we are in is worse than hell!!!" Finally, on June 17, the Senate approved the original bill by a nineteen to thirteen vote. The following day Madison signed the bill into law. The War of 1812 thus began on June 18, 1812.

The vote on the war bill—seventy-nine to forty-nine in the House and nineteen to thirteen in the Senate—was the closest vote on any formal declaration of war in American history. Only 61 percent of the members voting supported the bill. Most representatives and senators from Pennsylvania and the South and West voted for war, while most from the North and East voted against it. The sectional division was really a reflection of party strength, for the vote on the war bill was essentially a party vote. Some 81 percent of 121 Republicans in Congress voted for war, while all thirty-nine Federalists voted against it.

U.S. War Aims

What did the Republicans hope to accomplish with war? Their chief aim was to win concessions on the maritime issues, particularly the Orders-in-Council and impressment. Throughout the winter and spring of 1812, these issues had dominated almost every debate on American grievances, both in and out of Congress. In other words, war was undertaken primarily to secure "Free Trade and Sailors' Rights." The advocates of war also hoped to put an end to British influence over American Indians, but even in the West this issue took a back seat to the maritime issues because westerners blamed an agricultural depression on the Orders-in-Council.

Republicans saw the struggle as a second war of independence—a contest that would vindicate American sovereignty and preserve republican institutions by demonstrating to the world that the United States could uphold its rights. In addition, Republican leaders saw the war as a means of preserving power, unifying their party, and silencing their critics. Political considerations loomed large because (like the Federalists in 1798) most Republicans in 1812 identified the interests of their party with those of the nation. What was good for their party was considered good for the United States.

In sum, Republicans went to war in 1812 to achieve a variety of closely related diplomatic, ideological, and political objectives. The need to take some action was so urgent that Republicans did not wait for their war preparations to mature. This appalled some members of the party, but most were willing to take the risk. In the words of Congressman Robert Wright of Maryland, they were willing "to get married and buy the furniture afterwards."

Some Republicans—members of the "scarecrow" faction—hoped that no fighting would be necessary, that the British would respond to the declaration of war by caving in to American demands. Given the speed with which President Madison sent out peace feelers—within a week of the declaration of war—perhaps he, too, hoped for a bloodless victory. But even if the nation had to fight, Canada was considered an easy target. Americans could overrun the sparsely-populated country, and there would be little that the British could do about it because they were tied up in Europe 3,000 miles away.

The Washington *National Intelligencer* predicted that historians would rank the Twelfth Congress next to "the immortal Congress" of 1776. "Under the auspices of the one this nation sprung into existence; under those of the other it will have been preserved from disgraceful recolonization." The comparison to '76 was exaggerated, but it illustrated how potent the ideological legacy of the Revolution was and how difficult it was for Republicans to shed this baggage. For most Republicans, the War of 1812 was very much a second war of independence. But whether the young Republic could actually vindicate its independence against a foe as powerful as Great Britain remained to be seen.

Chapter 2

The Campaign of 1812

On December 16, 1811, after the debate on the war preparations had been under way for more than two weeks, John Randolph, an anti-war Republican, raised a specter that was to haunt contemporaries and historians alike. "Agrarian cupidity," he said, "not maritime right, urges the war. Ever since the report of the Committee on Foreign Relations came into the House, we have heard but one word—like the whip-poor-will, but one eternal monotonous tone—Canada! Canada! Canada!" Randolph exaggerated, since at no time during the debates did territorial expansion overshadow the maritime issues. Although territorial expansionism was a potent force in this era, the desire to conquer and annex Canada did not cause the war. "Canada was not the end but the means," said Henry Clay, "the object of the war being the redress of injuries, and Canada being the instrument by which that redress was to be obtained."

Targeting Canada

Most Republicans considered British Canada a logical target because it appeared to be so weak. About 7.7 million people lived in the United States, compared to only 500,000 in Canada. The Republic had only 12,000 regulars in uniform at the beginning of the war, but the enlistment of additional regulars, the recruitment of volunteers, and militia drafts were expected to swell that number dramatically. By contrast, Sir George Prevost, (pronounced Pray-vo) the forty-five-year-old governor-general of Canada, had only 10,000 regulars in Canada, and only 8,000 in Upper and Lower Canada (the modern provinces of Ontario and Quebec), where the fighting was expected to take place. Moreover, the loyalty of the population in Canada was suspect. The old French inhabitants felt little allegiance to the Crown, and the same could be said of the many recent American immigrants who had gone north to take advantage of generous land policies and low taxes.

Given the disparity between the United States and Canada, Henry Clay thought that "the militia of Kentucky are alone competent to place Montreal and Upper Canada at our feet." Thomas Jefferson was no less optimistic. "The acquisition of Canada this year, as far as the neighborhood of Quebec," he boasted, "will be a mere matter of marching, and will give us experience for the attack [on] Halifax the next [year] and the final expulsion of England from the American continent." Most Republicans expected what John Randolph called "a holiday campaign." With "no expense of blood, or treasure, on our part—Canada is to conquer herself—she is to be subdued by the principles of fraternity."

What would the United States do with Canada once it was conquered? This was unclear. Because the annexation of Canada was not the purpose of the war, presumably it would be returned for concessions on the maritime issues. But what if the British balked at concessions, or what if the American people were unwilling to part with territory once it was conquered? These were issues that U.S. officials never addressed, probably because the administration wanted to keep all of its options open.

Although the War Department instructed its commanders in the field to promise Canadians nothing more than protection for their persons, property, and rights, senior commanders in the field followed their own counsel. Two commanding officers, Brigadier General William Hull at Detroit and Brigadier General Alexander Smyth at Buffalo, issued proclamations that spoke openly of annexation. The administration's failure to publicly repudiate these proclamations made it all the more difficult to reconcile domestic opponents of the war or to deflect charges that this was a war of territorial expansion.

The War Department and Army

In spite of its advantages over Canada, the United States was ill-prepared to undertake a major war. The War Department, poorly organized and understaffed, was overwhelmed by the task of managing the war effort. The department's work load, heavy in time of peace, was staggering in time of war. "No man in the country," claimed one War Hawk, "is equal to one-half the duties which devolve on the present secretary." Although the department had eleven clerks, none had more than a year's experience, and the result was administrative chaos.

The secretary of war, William Eustis, was a Boston doctor who was a good politician, but he lacked administrative skills and never mastered his duties. Overwhelmed by the task before him, he frittered away time on details and sometimes corresponded with junior officers in the field while failing to give proper direction to senior officers.

"Our secretary of war," concluded a Pennsylvania congressman, "is a dead weight in our hands. . . . His unfitness is apparent to everybody but himself."

Conditions in the army were not much better. The senior officers, headed by two major generals and six brigadiers, inspired little confidence. Many owed their appointment to politics and lacked initiative or a taste for battle. According to Winfield Scott, "The old officers had, very generally, sunk into either sloth, ignorance, or habits of intemperate drinking." Although there were some promising junior officers, the new officers commissioned at the beginning of the war lacked military knowledge or experience. "Our army," complained War Hawk and militia brigadier Peter B. Porter in 1813, "is full of men, fresh from lawyer shops and counting rooms, who know little of the physical force of man—of the proper means of sustaining and improving it—or even the mode of its application."

The army was dominated by new recruits who lacked discipline and training, and even the more experienced enlisted men had no combat experience and were in any case stationed on the Gulf Coast, far from any active theater of operations during most of the war. There were numerous infractions of discipline, and these multiplied as the army grew. Desertion was so common that less than four months into the war President Madison felt obliged to issue a proclamation pardoning all who returned to duty.

The administration planned to rely on one-year volunteers, but only six regiments were raised, and one army officer claimed that those he inspected were little better than organized bandits who wasted public property, insulted private citizens, and freely engaged in "desertion, robbery, [and] disorderly and mutinous conduct." Except in New England and the West, the militia was poorly equipped, badly organized, and wholly undependable, and only in the West were citizen soldiers willing to serve on foreign territory. In short, the nation's land forces were not up to the task at hand.

Payment and Supply Problems

The system for paying the troops was hopelessly inefficient. At the start of the war, privates earned $5 a month, non-commissioned officers $7 to $9, and officers $20 to $200. To stimulate enlistments, Congress in late 1812 boosted the pay of privates and non-commissioned officers by $3. At $10 a month, privates still earned less than the $10 to $20 that unskilled laborers normally made, but steady increases in the enlistment bounty (which ultimately reached $124 and 320 acres of land) pushed army income far above the civilian average.

Even early in the war, when the administration had ample resources, few troops were paid on time. Communication was slow, administrative skills were uncommon, and moving money from one point to another was a challenge under the best of circumstances. In October 1812 men who had enlisted five months earlier "absolutely refused to march until they had received their pay," and other troops mutinied for want of pay. As the war progressed, the problem of paying the expanding army became almost unmanageable. By the fall of 1814 army pay was frequently six to twelve months in arrears, and in some cases even more.

The system of supply did not work much better. In March 1812 Congress re-established the quartermaster and commissary departments that had been abolished in an economy move in 1802, but it was months before either department was staffed and operational, and the authority granted to each was vague and overlapping. Throughout the war the system of supply was woefully inefficient, and troops in the field frequently had to go for months without shoes, clothing, blankets, or other vital supplies.

The system for feeding the troops, which was based on private contract, was even worse. It was "madness in the extreme," said one officer, to rely on such a system in time of war. The daily ration was supposed to consist of twenty ounces of beef or twelve ounces of pork; eighteen ounces of bread or flour; four ounces of rum, brandy, or whiskey (each of which had a much higher alcohol content than today); and small quantities of salt, vinegar, soap, and candles. Contractors and subcontractors, however, were often so intent on making profit that they delivered bad provisions or chiseled on the quantity.

Complaints about supply multiplied as the war progressed, and many illnesses and deaths were blamed on the system. Doubtless many agreed with Brigadier General Edmund P. Gaines that "the irregularity in the supply and badness of the rations" had done more to retard American operations than anything else. In fact, one U.S. general claimed that contractors knocked more men out of action than the enemy did, and another insisted the men were so badly supplied that the number killed in battle was "trifling" compared to losses from other causes.

American Weapons

The United States did a better job of equipping its soldiers with suitable weapons. There were well established arsenals at Springfield, Massachusetts, and Harpers Ferry, Virginia, and additional facilities were built during the war. The War Department was thus able to manufacture and repair small arms, produce ammunition, and test powder and ammunition. It also procured large guns, small arms, and powder from private manufacturers.

Congress created an ordnance department at the beginning of the war to oversee the procurement, testing, and management of artillery, and this agency functioned well. The main problem it faced was bringing order to the large variety of artillery and ammunition that had been acquired over the years from many domestic and foreign sources. The army's field artillery consisted mainly of conventional guns— mostly 3- to 12-pounders—that fired round shot (solid iron balls), canister (tin cans filled with musket balls), or grapeshot (canvas bags filled with iron balls usually the size of golf balls). Round shot was sometimes heated in a furnace into hot shot in the hope of torching an enemy structure. The army also had mortars and howitzers that fired explosive shells at an angle so that they could reach beyond earthworks and inside of forts.

Most enlisted men were issued the domestically manufactured Springfield Model 1795 musket. This was a .69-caliber muzzle-loaded weapon that fired a soft lead ball weighing about an ounce. It was accurate to a hundred yards but could be lethal at greater distances. Some soldiers, particularly in the West, were armed with rifles, which had a grooved barrel that gave the weapon greater range. Although some of these rifles were the Harpers Ferry Model 1803, most were privately manufactured to many different specifications in Pennsylvania (and thus were known as Pennsylvania rifles). Rifles fired smaller balls than muskets but were accurate up 200 yards and could be deadly at greater distances.

American Strategy in 1812

Given the state of the War Department and the army, the conquest of Canada was likely to be more difficult than Republicans imagined. Republicans also underestimated the enemy and the stupendous logistical problems the young Republic would have to overcome. The British army might be smaller than the U.S. Army, but its troops were better trained and disciplined and most of the officers were combat-tested. The British could also count on Indian allies, who were excellent scouts, trackers, and skirmishers and whose reputation for ferocity could tip the balance in any battle by panicking enemy soldiers.

Supplying an army so far from the centers of population was no easy task. Although the United States had shorter and more secure supply lines than the British (who had to ship almost everything overseas and then up the exposed St. Lawrence River), moving supplies from New York, Philadelphia, and Pittsburgh to the northern border was challenging. The roads were crude and the waterways undependable, and adverse weather could make moving freight difficult if not impossible.

Canada in this era was often compared to a tree. The tap roots were the sea lanes that connected Canada to the mother country; the trunk was the St. Lawrence River; and the branches were the outlying settlements on the Great Lakes or the waterways that drained into the lakes. Because the United States did not have a navy capable of severing the Canadian roots, it had to target the trunk, which meant assaulting Montreal and Quebec, the two cities that anchored British defenses on the St. Lawrence.

There was little enthusiasm for an immediate attack on Quebec. An assault on this city had failed in the American Revolution, and it lay deep in Canada and north of Federalist New England, which was unlikely to supply the men and material needed to support the campaign. This left Montreal, but concentrating on this city

The War in the North

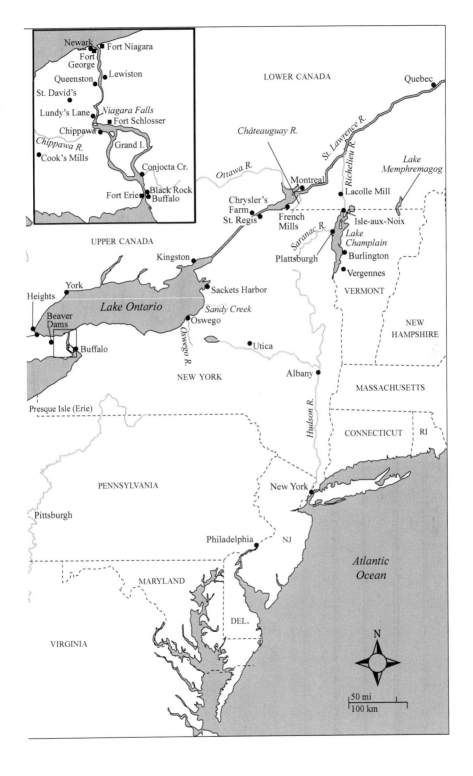

would not allow the administration to take advantage of the war enthusiasm in the West or to protect that region from Indian depredations. The president therefore adopted a plan developed by Major General Henry Dearborn that called for a three-pronged attack that targeted not only Montreal but also British positions on the Detroit and Niagara rivers. This, however, pushed the focus of American operations too far west and thus enabled the British to preserve their centers of power and population to the east.

Hull's Detroit Campaign

To oversee its operation in the West, the administration chose Brigadier General William Hull, the fifty-nine-year-old governor of the Michigan Territory. Hull had a solid record of service in the Revolutionary War, but age and ill-health had taken a heavy toll and he was ill-suited for a combat command. His men must have realized this because they nicknamed him "the old lady." Hull's orders, which were issued before the declaration of war, called for him to assemble an army in Ohio and march to Detroit.

After gathering some 2,000 men, Hull began the laborious task of cutting a road from Urbana, Ohio, to Detroit. It was slow going because he had to move through a wilderness wetland known as the Black Swamp. Arriving at the Maumee River at the end of June, he hired the schooner *Cuyahoga* to carry his papers, baggage, and medical supplies to Detroit. Although Hull did not yet know about the declaration of war, the British learned about it in time to seize the schooner as it moved up the Detroit River past Fort Amherstburg. This enabled them to learn about Hull's plan as well as the size and condition of his army.

Hull soon learned about the state of war and arrived at Detroit on July 5 without further incident. A week later he crossed the Detroit River into British territory with the intention of making an assault on Fort Amherstburg. Some 200 Ohio militiamen refused to accompany him, claiming they could not be forced to serve beyond American territory. The American invasion was followed by some inconclusive skirmishing. Hull then stopped to build carriages for his cannons. Although the delay cut into the morale of his troops, Hull's prospects still seemed bright. His force was larger than the British could muster, and a proclamation he had issued induced many Canadian militia to go home or to defect to the United States.

Hull's prospects, however, dimmed. The American commander became increasingly worried about his supply lines to Ohio, which were menaced from the Detroit River and Lake Erie by the British and from the surrounding forests by the Indians. Although 200 militiamen were en route from Ohio with supplies for Hull, they stopped at the River Raisin, some thirty-five miles south of Detroit. Hull sent several detachments to link up with the militia, but they either were ambushed by Indians or lost their way.

More bad news followed at the end of July when Hull learned that the small American outpost on the strategically located Mackinac Island between Lake Michigan and Lake Huron had fallen to an enemy force. Convinced that this "opened the northern hive of Indians" and that "they were swarming down in every direction," Hull ordered his men back to Detroit. "This fatal and unaccountable step," said one of his officers, "dispirited the troops" and "left to the tender mercy of the enemy the miserable Canadians who had joined us." At this point, Hull considered ordering his troops back to Ohio, but his senior officers warned that the army would disintegrate if he did.

The British made good use of Hull's reprieve. Major General Issac Brock arrived with reinforcements, and with the appearance of additional Indians, his combined force was about equal to Hull's. Brock also knew how demoralized Hull's army was because of a captured mailbag. "I got possession of the letters my antagonist addressed to the secretary of war," Brock said, "and also of the sentiments which hundreds of his army uttered to their friends. Confidence in the general was gone, and evident despondency prevailed throughout."

Crossing the river, Brock brought his big guns to bear on Fort Detroit, exchanging artillery fire with the Americans inside. Playing on Hull's fears of the Indians, Brock demanded surrender, telling the beleaguered American brigadier that once the fighting began in earnest, he would not be able to control his native allies. With many civilians in the fort (including members of his own family), Hull was horrified at the prospect of an Indian massacre. "My God!" he exclaimed to a subordinate, "What shall I do with these women and children?"

Facing a siege and the prospect of an Indian massacre, Hull became increasingly distracted and despondent. Finally, on August 16 he surrendered. "Not an officer was consulted," reported an army captain. "Even the women [were] indignant at the shameful degradation of the American character." Hull was taken to Quebec and then released on parole (which meant he could not fight again until exchanged). When he returned to the United States, a military court convicted him of cowardice and neglect of duty. The court sentenced him to death but recommended mercy because of his Revolutionary War service. Madison approved the verdict and remitted the punishment. Hull and his heirs spent the next thirty-five years trying (without much success) to salvage his reputation by vindicating his actions.

Several days before surrendering, Hull had ordered the evacuation of Fort Dearborn in Chicago on the grounds that the fall of Mackinac had rendered it vulnerable to an Indian attack. The fort was held by about sixty-five regulars and militia under Captain Nathan Heald. A couple of dozen civilians were also present. The post was well stocked, the nearby Indians were known to be unfriendly, and there was considerable opposition to evacuation. But Heald was determined to leave.

To pacify the Indians, Heald promised to turn over all his public stores, but he withheld the arms and liquor, which infuriated the Indians. On August 15, Heald marched out of the fort, ostensibly protected by some Miami Indians. Not far from the fort, the Miamis disappeared, and some 500 Indians, mostly Potawatomis under the leadership of Blackbird, attacked the Americans, killing many after surrender terms had been arranged. Captain William Wells, a "white Indian" who had once lived with the Miamis but now served as an Indian agent and interpreter, met a particularly grisly fate. The Indians beheaded him, carved out his heart, and ate it raw.

Harrison Takes Command

The loss of Mackinac, Detroit, and Chicago left much of the Old Northwest exposed to Indian depredations. The impact of these losses, said the Pittsburgh *Mercury*, was to lay open "to the ravages of the merciless foe the whole extent of our western frontier." Thrown into a panic, westerners fled from their farms and bombarded the government with demands for protection.

Government officials were eager to meet these demands, but it meant devoting scarce resources to a remote theater. The administration wanted to put the lackluster Brigadier General James Winchester in charge of the theater, but Kentucky made William Henry Harrison—the hero of Tippecanoe—a major general in the militia (even though he was not a resident of the state) and gave him command of all Kentucky troops. This forced the administration's hand, and it reluctantly put Harrison in charge of the western theater. Harrison spent the fall of 1812 building an army that soaked up federal money and supplies at an alarming rate.

Harrison's plan was to sweep hostile Indians from the region and retake Detroit. Although he targeted a number of Indian villages—most notably several belonging to the Miamis in Indiana Territory in the Battle of Mississinewa in mid-December—winter set in before he could move against Detroit.

To prepare winter quarters, Harrison sent Winchester to the rapids of the Maumee River. Following his own counsel, Winchester marched a force of 850 men to the River Raisin to protect Americans at Frenchtown (now Monroe, Michigan). Although he drove off the British, on January 22, 1813, Brigadier General Henry Procter counterattacked with an Anglo-Indian force of 1,100 men. In the Battle of Frenchtown, Winchester was captured and surrendered his entire force.

Fearing a larger American force was on the way, Procter retired to Fort Amherstburg with the walking wounded. The next day Indians killed some thirty of the American prisoners who remained behind. The Americans blamed the atrocity on the British. "The savages *were suffered to commit every depredation upon our wounded*," reported a group of American officers. "*Many were tomahawked, and many were burned alive in the houses.*" The story quickly spread, and soon "Remember the Raisin!" became a rallying cry throughout the West.

After a season of campaigning in the Old Northwest, the Republic had little to show for the blood and treasure expended. Sizeable armies had been lost at Detroit

This dramatic picture illustrates the Indian atrocities in the River Raisin Massacre. (William L. Clements Library, University of Michigan)

and Frenchtown; the forts at Mackinac, Detroit, and Dearborn were abandoned or in enemy hands; and Indian depredations continued unabated.

Van Rensselaer's Niagara Campaign

Further east U.S. military operations did not go much better. At the other end of Lake Erie, on the Niagara frontier, Major General Stephen Van Rensselaer of the New York militia was in charge. An influential Federalist landholder, the forty-seven-year-old Van Rensselaer was known as "the last of the patroons." He had no military experience and relied for guidance on his thirty-eight-year-old kinsman and aide, Colonel Solomon Van Rensselaer, who had fought in the Indian wars of the 1790s and had long served as adjutant general of the New York militia. The elder Van Rensselaer shared his command in western New York with forty-seven-year-old Brigadier General Alexander Smyth of the regular army. Vain and pompous, Smyth had written a tactical guide but was without practical military experience. Although the War Department ordered him to cooperate with Van Rensselaer, Smyth refused to do so.

By October 1812 there were about 6,400 American troops facing perhaps 2,300 British and Indians across the Niagara River. Van Rensselaer's plan was to target

Queenston Heights with his force while Smyth assaulted Fort George. But Smyth, unwilling to take orders from a militia officer, remained aloof and uncooperative. Van Rensselaer had a numerical advantage even without Smyth's 1,600 troops, and, fearing public criticism if he remained inactive, he decided to attack Queenston anyway.

The attack was planned for October 11 but had to be postponed when a boat carrying the oars for the other boats disappeared down the river. The crossing was made two days later by 300 men, mostly regulars, led by Colonel Solomon Van Rensselaer. Van Rensselaer was wounded several times, and his men found themselves pinned down at the river bank. Captain John E. Wool took command and led the men up a fisherman's path to the heights above. The British were driven off, and soon 600 Americans, now under the command of Lieutenant Colonel Winfield Scott, had taken control of the heights. Major General Brock, who had returned from Detroit, was killed in a British counterattack.

While the British prepared for a fresh counterattack, the Americans were pinned down by a group of Grand River Iroquois led by Mohawk leader John Norton. The Americans desperately needed reinforcements, and Major General Van Rensselaer ordered the New York militiamen to cross over, but they refused. Although most were "violent Democrats" who supported the war, they were disheartened by the Indian war whoops they heard and by the killed and wounded who were ferried back from the Canadian side. Hence, they claimed they could not be forced to serve outside the country.

Without reinforcements, Scott men's could not hold their ground against a determined British counterattack. Some 925, including Scott, were forced to surrender. Local Republicans, who were never reconciled to Van Rensselaer's command, claimed that because he was a Federalist he had tipped the British off in advance of the attack.

After the disaster, Van Rensselaer asked to be relieved, and the War Department, unaware of Smyth's liabilities, put him in charge. Smyth planned an assault against Fort Erie at the southern end of the Niagara River but wasted time composing bombastic proclamations that even the British found laughable. Known to his men as "Van Bladder" and "Alexander the Great," Smyth sounded more like a postman than a soldier when he told his troops, "Neither rain, snow, or frost will prevent the embarkation." Although a preliminary attack destroyed some British positions across the river, Smyth gave up the main attack when his officers voted it down, partly because the Pennsylvania militia units made it clear that they would not cross over.

Abandoning the attack on Fort Erie brought the campaign on the Niagara to an end. The only thing gained was the death of Brock, a military genius whose loss the Quebec *Gazette* called "a public calamity." As for Smyth, he was bitterly assailed by the New York militia, and several citizen soldiers fired their muskets into his tent. He returned to his home in Virginia and was dropped from the army's rolls in a re-organization in 1813.

Dearborn's Montreal Campaign

The third prong of the invasion should have been the most important but actually amounted to the least. This was the attack on Montreal that was supposed to be carried out by sixty-one-year old Major General Henry Dearborn, who had fought in the Revolution and served as Jefferson's secretary of war. But Dearborn, like Hull, had no taste for battle and no desire to spend time in the field campaigning. Nicknamed by his men "Granny," he preferred to linger in New England and New York, overseeing recruiting and the construction of defenses. Finally, the War Department ordered him to launch his campaign.

Dearborn planned to give the field command to Brigadier General Joseph Bloomfield, a political appointee who was governor of New Jersey, but when the latter became ill, Dearborn had little choice but to assume control himself. Still, it was November before he marched his army, a mixed force of 6,000 regulars and militia, from Plattsburgh, New York, to the Canadian frontier.

Colonel Zebulon Pike secured permission from Dearborn to lead a detachment of 500 men to attack a band of Indians who were thought to be nearby. Pike did not find the Indians, but he attacked a British outpost at Lacolle Mill on November 20. The Battle of Lacolle Mill was inconclusive, and in the darkness and confusion American units exchanged fire. By now Dearborn realized that most of his militia would not cross the border, and he used this as an excuse to call off the campaign and return to Plattsburgh. A Republican later described Dearborn's failure as a "miscarriage without even [the] heroism of disaster."

The Failure of American Arms

The U.S. invasion of Canada in 1812 had failed on all three fronts. The campaign, said a Republican newspaper, had produced "disaster, defeat, disgrace, and ruin and death." U.S. armies had surrendered at Detroit, Frenchtown, and Queenston; much of the Old Northwest was either in enemy hands or subject to Indian raids; and no headway had been made against the critical British city of Montreal on the St. Lawrence.

The main reason for the failure was poor leadership. The administration's strategy was unfocused and poured too many resources into the West; the War Department failed to give timely and appropriate direction to commanders in the field; and the commanders themselves were not up to the job. Some of the junior officers, like Winfield Scott, John Wool, and Zebulon Pike, had shown promise; and the enlisted men had proven adequate, although most lacked the training and discipline they needed. As for citizen soldiers, they had been a major disappointment. When forced to take the offensive, more often than not they had proven undisciplined, unreliable, and unwilling to leave the country.

The entire campaign demonstrated the toll that a decade of Jeffersonian par-simony had taken on the military establishment and the difficulty of building an effective army overnight. "The degraded state in which the military institutions have been retained," concluded the Philadelphia *Aurora,* "comes now upon us with a dismal sentence of retribution."

Uncle Sam's First Appearance

One byproduct of the campaign that would loom large in the future was the first appearance of the nickname "Uncle Sam." On December 23, 1812, the Bennington (Vermont) *News-Letter* published a letter from a Federalist who had been drafted into militia duty. "Now, Mr. Editor," the conscripted citizen soldier asked, "pray if you can inform me, what single solitary good thing will, or can accrue to (Uncle Sam) the U.S. for all the expense, marching and countermarching, pain, sickness, death &c. among us?"

This was the first known allusion to "Uncle Sam." References to "Uncle Sam" proliferated during the war. They usually carried a negative connotation, and some-times they referred to the U.S. Army rather than the government or nation. By the end of the war, however, this nickname (which did not yet conjure up a visual image) was well on its way to achieving special status in the American lexicon.

The Rival Navies

The war at sea went better for the United States but not because of superior leader-ship in the cabinet. The secretary of the navy was Paul Hamilton, a South Carolina rice planter with little knowledge of naval affairs. Hamilton was an alcoholic who was sometimes drunk by noon, and one Republican said that he was "about as fit for his place as the Indian Prophet would be for Emperor of Europe." Hamilton's one claim to his office was that he was a proponent of naval expansion.

A decade of Republican neglect had taken a heavy toll on the navy, but seventeen ships still survived in 1812. Seven were frigates. The *Constitution, President,* and *United States* were rated at 44 guns; the *Constellation, Chesapeake,* and *Congress* at 36 guns; and the *Essex* at 32 guns. Another frigate, the *Adams,* was being cut down to a corvette and would eventually go to war as a sloop-of-war. There were also nine smaller vessels rated at 10 to 20 guns. American naval commanders loved firepower, and most of the ships that went to sea were crammed with extra guns. Some of the ships also carried extra crewmen.

The frigates were the heart of the navy. Designed by Philadelphia shipwright Joshua Humphreys, the three heavy frigates—known as "44s"—were longer and sturdier than conventional frigates. They carried heavier guns—24-pounders instead of 18-pounders—as their main battery, and they had thicker hulls. They were also pretty good sailers. In truth, they were "super-frigates," capable of out-fighting and out-sailing other frigates and of outrunning anything larger.

The Republic also had the advantage of a rich maritime tradition. The bulk of the population lived on or near the eastern seaboard, and many Americans made their living off the sea. Those in the navy often had learned seamanship on merchant ships. Many had seen action in the Quasi-War (1798–1801) or the Tripolitan War (1801–1805), and some had served on British warships. Even those without combat experience were skilled marksmen with great guns (cannons) and small arms because of constant practice. Unlike the British navy, which had to depend on impressment, the U.S. Navy relied exclusively on volunteers, and the morale of the service was high. In addition, the navy did not face the same logistical problems as the army. The fleet was small, and once supplied a ship could remain at sea for months.

In spite of its high morale, the navy had trouble keeping its ships fully manned. The army siphoned off potential recruits (some with considerable naval experience) because of the ever increasing bounties it offered. The competition from privateers was even keener. Privateering was an attractive alternative to seamen because the tour of duty was shorter (typically just two or three months), the prospect of an armed engagement less, and the chances of large profits greater.

The usual term of service for the navy was a year, and normally there was no bounty. The pay ranged from $6 a month for boys and landsmen without any experience at sea to $20 for sail makers. Most seamen could earn more on a merchantman and a lot more on a lucky privateer. To compete, the navy found that it had to offer incentives, including a bounty (ranging from $10 to $30), three months' advance pay, and a 25 percent boost in pay. These incentives went a long way toward getting the men needed for oceangoing cruises, but recruiting for gunboat service on the coast or for inland service on the lakes remained difficult.

Even when it was fully manned, the tiny American fleet hardly seemed a match for the Mistress of the Seas. For more than a century, Great Britain had ruled the waves, and its naval superiority was overwhelming. The Royal Navy had over 500 ships in service, including 115 ships-of-the-line (the battleships of the day) and 126 frigates. But these were scattered all over the world, performing blockade, convoy, and patrol service, and Britain could ill-afford to divert them to America. At the beginning of the war, there were only twenty-five warships assigned to the Halifax station: one small ship-of-the-line, five frigates, and nineteen smaller vessels. Although additional ships were assigned to the Newfoundland and West Indian stations, they could not be spared from other duties.

The Royal Navy faced other problems. Its manpower needs had soared from 45,000 in 1793 to 145,000 in 1812, which meant that most of its ships were chronically undermanned. A lack of skilled workers and materials at the navy yards in Halifax and Bermuda meant that ships in need of a major overhaul had to be sent home. In addition, after its great victory over a combined French and Spanish fleet at Trafalgar in 1805, the Admiralty prohibited live-fire training to save on gun powder, and this undermined the readiness of the gun crews.

American Naval Strategy in 1812

American officials planned to send the navy to sea in two squadrons (later increased to three) with orders "to afford to our returning commerce all possible protection." But this order arrived after Captain John Rodgers, who was in charge of one of the squadrons that included the U.S. frigate *President* (54 guns), had already set sail in search of a rich convoy that was headed for England from Jamaica. Although he never found the convoy, his cruise had an impact on British strategy.

On June 23, 1812, Rodgers's squadron exchanged fire with the British frigate *Belvidera* (42 guns). This was the first engagement of the war. The *Belvidera* escaped and made it to Halifax, with the news of war and of the presence of Rodgers's squadron off the American coast. Vice Admiral Herbert Sawyer, who was in command of the Halifax station, considered posting a single ship in front of each American port to intercept returning American merchantmen but feared that Rodgers's squadron might pick off his ships one at a time. Hence, he kept his own squadron concentrated and sent it in search of Rodgers's. "We have been so completely occupied looking for Commodore Rodgers' squadron," said a British naval officer, "that we have taken very few prizes."

Although the Royal Navy captured a fair number of American merchantmen, Sawyer's caution enabled most to reach home safely with whatever cargo they had aboard. The windfall for the United States was considerable. The flood of imports replenished the nation's stockpile of goods and boosted the customs revenue. In addition, the return of so many seamen expanded the pool of labor available to fill out the crews of warships and privateers that were fitting out for sea.

The *Constitution*'s Success

Some American warships cruised alone in 1812, and their record was impressive. In July Captain Isaac Hull, the nephew of the disgraced army general, had command of the U.S. frigate *Constitution* when it outran the Halifax squadron in a remarkable fifty-seven-hour chase that showcased the skills of American seamen. Both sides marveled at Hull's feat, even the British conceding that it was "elegant."

After taking on supplies at Boston, Hull returned to the sea. On August 19 about 700 miles east of Boston, the *Constitution* (carrying 55 guns) encountered the British frigate *Guerrière* (49 guns), commanded by Captain James R. Dacres (pronounced Da-kers) and described by the *Naval Chronicle* as "one of our stoutest frigates." After outmaneuvering the *Guerrière*, Hull delivered a powerful and destructive raking

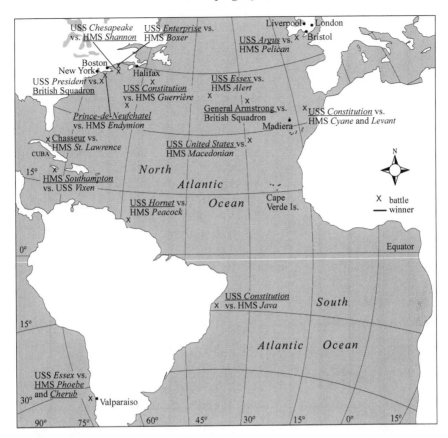

USS *Chesapeake* USS *Enterprise* vs. Liverpool• •London
vs. HMS *Shannon* HMS *Boxer*
USS *Argus* vs. X Bristol
HMS *Pelican*

Boston
New York• X Halifax USS *Essex* vs.
USS *President* vs. X HMS *Alert*
British Squadron USS *Constitution*
vs. HMS *Guerrière* X
X
General Armstrong vs. X USS *Constitution* vs.
Prince-de-Neufchatel British Squadron HMS *Cyane* and *Levant*
vs. HMS *Endymion* Madiera •

X *Chasseur* vs.
HMS *St. Lawrence* USS *United States* vs. X
CUBA HMS *Macedonian*
N
15° X *North*
HMS *Southampton*
vs. USS *Vixen* *Atlantic*
X battle
USS *Hornet* vs. *Ocean* Cape — winner
HMS *Peacock* Verde Is.
X

0° Equator

USS *Constitution* *South*
X vs. HMS *Java*

15° *Atlantic Ocean*

USS *Essex* vs.
HMS *Phoebe*
30° and *Cherub* X •Valparaiso
90° 75° 60° 45° 30° 15° 0° 15°

The War at Sea

fire that swept the deck of the British ship. An American on board the British ship said the *Constitution's* double-shotted first fire (700 pounds of metal delivered at close range) sounded like "a tremendous explosion" and forced the *Guerrière* to "reel and tremble as though she had received the shock of an earthquake."

Although the *Guerrière* returned fire, its masts were soon destroyed, its hull damaged, and most of its crew knocked out of action. This left Dacres with little choice but to surrender. Unable to salvage the British ship, Hull removed its crew and ordered it set afire and sent to the bottom. During the battle an American tar who had seen a round shot bounce off the hull of the *Constitution* exclaimed, "Huzza! Her sides are made of iron." Thereafter, the ship was known affectionately as "Ironsides" and soon "Old Ironsides."

On December 29, 1812, off the coast of Brazil, the *Constitution,* now under the command of Captain William Bainbridge and carrying 54 guns, encountered the

British frigate *Java,* commanded by Captain Henry Lambert and carrying 49 guns. Both commanders demonstrated excellent seamanship, but once again superior firepower and marksmanship carried the day for the United States. American gunners destroyed most of the *Java's* rigging and killed or wounded a large portion of the British crew. Unable to maneuver, *Java* surrendered. After removing the crew and passengers (which included a lieutenant general who was headed for a command in India), Bainbridge sent the British hulk to the bottom.

Other Naval Victories

On October 25, 1812, the U.S. frigate *United States,* carrying 56 guns and commanded by Captain Stephen Decatur, was cruising 600 miles west of the Canaries when it encountered a British frigate, the *Macedonian,* carrying 49 guns and commanded by Captain John S. Carden. Although the *United States* was known as "the Wagon" because she was such a poor sailer, Decatur took advantage of his long guns and his crew's marksmanship. The *United States* got off seventy broadsides, the *Macedonian* only thirty. According to a seaman on the British ship, "Grapeshot and

The *United States,* under the command of Captain Stephen Decatur, won America's second victory over a British frigate, in this case the *Macedonian.* (Engraving by Benjamin Tanner based on a painting by Thomas Birch. Library of Congress)

canister were pouring through our portholes like leaden hail; the large shot came against ship's side, shaking her to the very keel, and passing through her timbers and scattering terrific splinters, which did more appalling work than the shot itself."

By the time the British ship got close enough to the *United States* to use its guns effectively, it had lost most of its spars and rigging and a third of its crew, forcing Carden to strike his colors. When Decatur boarded the vessel, he found "fragments of the dead scattered in every direction, the decks slippery with blood, [and] one continuous agonizing yell of the unhappy wounded." The *Macedonian* was repaired and then a prize crew sailed her into Newport Harbor, the only time a British frigate has ever been brought into an American port as a prize of war.

Several smaller U.S. warships also distinguished themselves. The U.S. sloop *Wasp* (18 guns) defeated the British sloop *Frolic* (22 guns), the U.S. sloop *Hornet* (20 guns) out-dueled the British sloop *Peacock* (20 guns), and the American frigate *Essex* (which was overloaded with 46 guns) beat the British brig *Alert* (18 guns?). Although the Royal Navy captured three American warships—the *Wasp, Nautilus* (14 guns), and *Vixen* (14 guns)—the balance was clearly in favor of the United States.

In all, the U.S. Navy had defeated three British frigates and four smaller vessels while losing only three small vessels of its own. American success was due to the superiority of the heavy frigates and the skillful seamanship and gunnery displayed on all the ships.

The War on Commerce

The U.S. Navy captured fifty enemy merchant vessels early in the war, but the real damage to British commerce was done by American privateers. Known as "the militia of the sea," privateers were merchant vessels that were chosen for their speed and armed under government authority so that they could cruise against the enemy's commerce. American privateers took 450 prizes in the first six months of the war. "*Jonathan's* privateers," complained a British correspondent, using a common expression for Americans, "have roved with impunity and success to all corners of the earth."

Although a lot of small privateers were sent to sea early in the war, the most successful cruises were made by large, heavily armed and well-manned ships that scoured the Atlantic. The *Yankee* (15 guns), sailing out of Bristol, Rhode Island, took eight British vessels valued at $300,000, and the *Rossie* (15 guns), commanded by Joshua Barney of Baltimore, captured eighteen vessels worth close to $1.5 million.

The Royal Navy did what it could to track down American privateers, and it captured 150 of them in the first six months of the war. The British navy also targeted any American merchantmen bold enough to venture to sea. So, too, did British privateers, some cruising from ports in the British Isles, others from Halifax and other ports in Canada.

Impact of American Success at Sea

American success in the war at sea gave a tremendous boost to domestic morale, a boost that was sorely needed because the nation was reeling from the disasters on the Canadian frontier. "Our brilliant naval victories," said an army officer, "serve, in some measure, to wipe out the disgrace brought upon the nation by the conduct of our generals." There was also considerable pride in humbling the Mistress of the Seas in her own element. "British arms cannot withstand American upon the sea," exulted a Republican congressman. "The bully has been disgraced by an infant."

The British were stunned by their losses. In more than two hundred naval engagements with France and her allies over a twenty-year period, the British had lost only four times. Against the U.S. Navy, by contrast, they had lost five times in a row, including three engagements that involved frigates. Although the London *Times* acknowledged the merits of American ships and seamen, the more common view was expressed by the London *Evening Standard,* which characterized the U.S. Navy as "a few fir-built frigates manned by a handful of bastards and outlaws." Given this contempt, the American victories went down hard. "It is a cruel mortification," said a cabinet official, "to be beat by these second-hand Englishmen upon our own element."

Since the more powerful ship prevailed in just about every engagement, the British need not have fretted. Still, the official view circulated in Great Britain was that the heavy U.S. frigates were actually ships-of-the-line in disguise manned by "picked" crews consisting mainly of British tars. None of this was true. More practically, the Admiralty dispatched additional warships to the New World and launched a crash program to build heavy frigates. It also secretly ordered British frigates not to cruise alone or "to engage, single-handed, the larger class of American ships, which, though they may be called frigates . . . [resemble] line-of-battle ships." The government also wisely ordered all British merchantmen in the Atlantic to sail in convoy with an armed escort.

Outcome of the Campaign

The outcome of the campaign of 1812 was a surprise to people on both sides of the Atlantic. The conquest of Canada, which was supposed to be (in Jefferson's words) "a mere matter of marching," had eluded the United States, while the war at sea, in which the British were supposed to have a decisive advantage, had gone surprisingly well for the young Republic. Both sides had been unprepared for the war, and this had worked to Britain's advantage in Canada but to America's on the high seas.

Time, however, was on Britain's side. In June 1812 Napoleon had marched one of the largest armies ever assembled, some 600,000 men, into Russia. By the fall of 1812 stout resistance and a lack of supplies had forced him to retreat. The retreat had turned into a rout, and by the end of the year Napoleon's Grand Army had melted away. If Napoleon's fortunes continued to wane, the British would be able to devote more military and naval resources to the American war, which would significantly reduce any chance that the United States had of conquering Canada or the winning any maritime concessions. For the young Republic, in other words, time was running out.

Chapter 3

The Campaign of 1813

When the spring thaw opened the campaigning season in 1813, the United States was better able to wage war than it had been in 1812. Two cabinet changes helped. John Armstrong had replaced William Eustis as secretary of war, and William Jones had succeeded Paul Hamilton as secretary of the navy. Although Armstrong was an intriguer who was disliked by everyone else in the cabinet, he was a decided improvement over Eustis, and Jones proved to be a first-class administrator who not only managed the nation's limited naval resources efficiently but also handled the prickly personalities in the naval officer corps with a firm hand.

There was also improved leadership in the field. William Henry Harrison had emerged as a leader in the Old Northwest, and Andrew Jackson would soon make his mark in the Old Southwest. Other leaders on the northern frontier, such as Winfield Scott, Zebulon Pike, and Jacob Brown, were also beginning to make their mark. Training and combat experience improved the men in the ranks, too.

Although enlistments lagged behind need, a combination of better pay and higher bounties attracted more men to the service. By the spring of 1813, there were 30,000 men in uniform. This was more than twice the number that the nation had at the beginning of the war and 50 percent more than the 20,000 regulars and quasi-regulars that British could now muster in Canada.

American Strategy in 1813

American strategy once again focused on targets in Upper Canada. Quebec was again ignored, and even Montreal was considered too well defended to be a primary target. Although Armstrong had trouble setting priorities, his plan was to regain control of the Old Northwest, drive the British from the Niagara Peninsula, and destroy

Britain's two naval bases on Lake Ontario (Kingston and York). Success against these targets was expected to pave the way for operations against Montreal and other British positions further east.

The key to the campaign was control of the Great Lakes, particularly Ontario and Erie. Because of the dense wilderness and lack of good roads, the lakes offered the most efficient means of moving men and material along the northern frontier. Whoever controlled the lakes controlled the whole border region.

At the beginning of the war, the British had undisputed command of both lakes, which had played a central role in their success in 1812. Brock had been able to move men and material back and forth over Lake Erie to ensure victory at both Detroit and Queenston. Americans were aware of how important control of the lakes was but in 1812 had hoped that a few well-delivered strokes would enable them to destroy British power in Upper Canada and thus render the whole question academic.

After Hull's defeat, the administration was determined to secure control over the lakes. "The success of the ensuing campaign," said the secretary of the navy, "will depend absolutely upon our superiority on all the Lakes, and every effort and resource must be directed to that object." Accordingly, in September 1812 the Navy Department ordered Captain Isaac Chauncey, a forty-year-old veteran officer, "to assume command of the naval force on lakes Erie and Ontario, and to use every exertion to obtain control of them this fall."

The nation already had a naval base at Sackets Harbor, New York, on Lake Ontario, and Chauncey dispatched Lieutenant Jesse Elliott to develop a shipyard at Black Rock (near Buffalo) for Lake Erie. At the same time the Navy Department sent Sailing Master Daniel Dobbins to develop a second yard at Presque Isle in Pennsylvania, and this soon became the principal base on Lake Erie. By purchasing merchant vessels and converting them into small warships and by launching an energetic program to build additional warships, American officials hoped to wrest control of both lakes from the British.

British officials fully appreciated the significance of the U.S. challenge but found it difficult to match the American building program because they had to ship their men and equipment across the Atlantic and over a long and exposed Canadian water route. Moreover, for the first nine months of the war British warships on the lakes were under the direction of the Provincial Marine, an army transport service staffed by men who were old and ill-equipped for energetic action. Not until March 1813 did London put Sir James Yeo (pronounced Yo), a Royal Navy captain who was given the rank of commodore, in charge, and not until 1814 did the Royal Navy assume responsibility for the ships. In spite of these liabilities, the British managed to maintain parity on Lake Ontario. On Lake Erie, however, they lacked the manpower and resources to keep pace.

The Invasion of Ohio

When the campaigning season opened in the spring of 1813, the British still controlled Lake Erie and thus remained on the offensive in the Old Northwest. Britain's Indian allies were eager to invade the United States, and Brigadier General Henry Procter wanted to act before the Americans became too strong. Accordingly, in late April Procter sailed from Fort Amherstburg with 1,000 regulars and militia for the mouth of the Maumee, where he rendezvoused with Tecumseh and 1,200 Indians. Their target was Fort Meigs, an exceptionally well-fortified post (in present-day Perrysburg) that was defended by 1,100 men under Harrison's command. Despite an artillery-backed siege that lasted from May 1 to May 9, the fort held out, and Procter withdrew, although not before mauling a 1,200-man relief force under Brigadier General Green Clay on May 5. The Indians killed some forty American prisoners of war before Tecumseh and British Indian Agent Matthew Elliott intervened to end the slaughter.

In July, Procter (who was now a major general) invaded Ohio to target Fort Meigs again. This time Procter had 500 regulars and a large body of Indians. Following a plan developed by Tecumseh, the British hoped to lure the Americans out of Fort Meigs, which was now under the command of Green Clay, by staging a sham battle nearby. When the ruse failed, Procter marched to Fort Stephenson, thirty miles to the southeast, in what today is Fremont, Ohio.

Fort Stephenson was defended by 160 men under the command of Major George Croghan (pronounced Crawn), who was only twenty-one years old. The Indians who accompanied Procter had no taste for assaulting a fortified position and melted away before the battle, which took place on August 1–2. When the British reached a ditch near the fort, they were cut down by fire from small arms and a concealed cannon known as "Good Bess." Calling this "the severest fire I ever saw," Procter gave up the assault and returned to Canada.

Balance of Power on Lake Erie

Procter's second invasion of Ohio ended British offensive operations in the Old Northwest because by then the balance of power on Lake Erie was shifting against them. The previous October, Lieutenant Jesse Elliott, who was still in command at Black Rock, launched a daring and successful night raid to capture two British vessels, the *Detroit* (6 guns) and *Caledonia* (3 guns), that were anchored adjacent to Fort Erie. Although the *Detroit* had to be burned when it ran aground, Elliott got the *Caledonia* safely to the American side of the river. Since the *Detroit* was loaded with war material taken in the capture of Detroit, this was a significant loss to the British.

By the end of 1812 Chauncey was looking for a more seasoned officer to take command on Lake Erie. He chose twenty-seven-year-old Master Commandant

Oliver H. Perry, who was looking for a way to escape from the gunboat duty he had been assigned to at Newport, Rhode Island. Perry's task when he arrived on the Niagara in the spring of 1813 was to move the five vessels at Black Rock to Presque Isle (one hundred miles away) and then to complete the four vessels that were under construction at Presque Isle. By August Perry's squadron of nine vessels, headed by two twenty-gun brigs, the *Lawrence* and *Niagara*, was ready for action. In early September Perry sailed his squadron to Put-in-Bay, located in the Bass Islands at the western end of Lake Erie, so that he could monitor the British squadron and disrupt the British supply line that extended across the lake to Fort Amherstburg.

The British had been working to expand their own squadron on the lake but had trouble getting the materials they needed to the navy yard at Fort Amherstburg. They also had trouble securing enough provisions to feed both the British army stationed at the fort and the huge band of Indians camped there. The officer in charge of the British squadron was Commander Robert H. Barclay, who had served with Admiral Horatio Nelson and lost an arm in the service (which prompted the Indians to refer to him as "our father with one arm"). Barclay had only six ships in his squadron with decidedly less firepower than Perry. But to keep his supply lines open, he decided "to risk everything," and on September 9 he set sail to meet Perry's squadron.

The Battle of Lake Erie

On September 10, 1813, the two squadrons clashed near South Bass Island. Perry had made the *Lawrence* (20 guns) his flagship while assigning command of the *Niagara* (20 guns) to Elliott. To take advantage of his superior firepower, Perry ordered his ships to close, but for reasons that have never been satisfactorily explained, Elliott held back. The *Lawrence* repeatedly exchanged broadsides with the two largest British ships, the *Detroit* (19 guns), which was Barclay's flagship, and the *Queen Charlotte* (17 guns). After two hours of fighting, all three ships were badly damaged, and the casualties on both sides staggering. Perry's crew had suffered more than 80 percent casualties, forcing the commander to call up the surgeon's assistants and walking wounded from below to man his guns.

Although his ship had become a floating hulk, Perry refused to surrender. Instead, he hauled down his battle flag, hopped into a small boat manned by four unwounded sailors, and headed for the *Niagara*, miraculously escaping injury from the rain of fire around him. Taking command of the *Niagara*, Perry sailed back into the heart of the British squadron. The two main British ships tried to wind around to bring fresh batteries into action, but in the process the *Queen Charlotte* rammed the *Detroit*, rendering both ships immobile. Aided by two of his schooners, Perry pounded the British ships into submission.

Three hours into the battle, the larger British ships had been destroyed, and the first and second in command on all six British ships had been killed or wounded.

Barclay, his good arm now mangled, had been carried below with multiple wounds. Unable to offer further resistance, four of the British ships surrendered. Two tried to escape but were run down and forced to surrender, too.

Perry's triumph on Lake Erie was a tribute to his courage and coolness under fire and to the effective use of his superior firepower. He now added more luster to his name by sending Major General Harrison one of the most famous after-action reports in history. "We have met the enemy and they are ours: two ships, two brigs, one schooner, and one sloop." Perry's victory was the most important on the Great Lakes during the war. It changed the balance of power on Lake Erie and enabled the United States to recover all that it had lost the previous year.

With his supply lines to the Detroit River severed, Major General Procter ordered a pullback to the east. Britain's Indian allies, who wanted to make a stand in defense of their lands, were furious. Tecumseh publicly compared Procter to "a fat animal that carries its tail upon its back but when affrighted . . . drops it between his legs and runs off." But the only concession he could win from Procter was a promise to make a stand somewhere to the east of Detroit.

Meanwhile, Perry repaired his ships so that he could transport men and supplies for an American offensive, while Harrison raised additional troops, mainly in Kentucky. Among the recruits were 1,200 mounted Kentucky volunteers led by congressional War Hawk and militia colonel Richard M. Johnson. With the new recruits, Harrison had about 5,500 men. With Perry's aid, the army moved to the Detroit River, occupying Fort Detroit and Fort Amherstburg. Although 150 Pennsylvania militiamen refused to cross into Canada, the Kentuckians had no such qualms. Harrison now began his pursuit of Procter. Although he never expected to catch up with the British, Procter's retreat was leisurely, and he left most of the bridges he crossed intact so that his straggling Indian allies could follow. Harrison's men soon came across baggage and supplies discarded by the British. They also captured two gunboats on the Thames River that were carrying Procter's spare ammunition.

The Battle of the Thames

With Harrison closing in, Procter decided to make a stand on the Thames near Moraviantown, about fifty miles east of Detroit. Procter had only 800 regulars (and only 600 fit for service), and he arrayed them in open order in two thin lines extending from the river to a large swamp. Britain's Indian allies, perhaps 500 warriors headed by Tecumseh, took up positions in the underbrush near the swamp and thus anchored Procter's right flank.

On October 5 Harrison approached with some 3,000 troops, including 1,000 of Johnson's mounted volunteers. Johnson asked to make a frontal assault with his men. Although this kind of cavalry charge was unusual, Harrison believed that "American backwoodsmen ride better in the woods than any other people" and thus consented. Shouting "Remember the Raisin!" Johnson's troops, divided into two wings, galloped toward the British and Indians. Led by Johnson's brother, the right wing burst through the British lines, dismounted, and after a brief exchange, captured almost the entire British force.

Richard Johnson led the left wing of the cavalry charge against the Indians. Although he sustained several wounds, Johnson rallied enough to kill an approaching Indian, probably Tecumseh. This feat helped catapult Johnson into the vice presidency in 1836. Although they resisted for a half hour longer than the British, the Indians disappeared into the forest once word spread that Tecumseh was dead.

The Kentuckians returned to the battlefield the next day and, with the aid of several captured British officers, identified Tecumseh's swollen corpse. His clothing, hair, and even patches of his skin were taken for souvenirs. "I [helped] kill Tecumseh and [helped] *skin him,*" a veteran of the campaign remembered a half century later, "and brought two pieces of his yellow hide home with me to my mother and sweethearts." Although Procter escaped with some of his men, a military court found him guilty of mismanaging his retreat. He was reprimanded and was never given another command.

The Battle of the Thames (known in Canada as the Battle of Moraviantown) was an important victory for the United States. Although the casualties on both sides were light, the Americans captured 600 British soldiers as well as a large quantity of

This dramatic rendition of the Battle of the Thames shows Richard M. Johnson killing the great Shawnee leader Tecumseh. (Lithograph by John Dorival. Library of Congress)

war material. Coupled with Perry's victory on Lake Erie, the Battle of the Thames turned the tide in the Old Northwest and secured the region for the United States. With the United States now in the ascendant, many (but not all) of the Indian tribes defected from the British and either sat out the rest of the war or fought alongside the Americans.

The Contest on Lake Ontario

There was little action on Lake Ontario in 1812 because the United States did not have enough ships to challenge the British for control. Thereafter the balance tipped back and forth depending on the progress of the building programs at Kingston and Sackets Harbor. But because the opposing commanders—Chauncey and Yeo—were both cautious men, unwilling to risk a battle without a clear advantage, there was no decisive naval engagement on Lake Ontario.

The closest that the opposing squadrons came to a major battle occurred on September 28, 1813, about twelve miles south of York. News had just arrived of Perry's victory on Lake Erie, and this was a rare occasion when both Chauncey and Yeo were willing to risk an engagement at the same time. In the ensuing clash, fire from Chauncey's flagship, the *General Pike* (28 guns), damaged Yeo's flagship, the *Wolfe* (21 guns), and Yeo's squadron fled west toward Burlington Heights fifteen miles away with Chauncey in hot pursuit. For ninety minutes the two squadrons raced across the lake, driven by gale force winds, and occasionally exchanging fire. As Yeo neared a bar in Burlington Bay, Chauncey, fearing that the fierce winds might drive his ships ashore or expose them to land-based artillery fire, gave up his pursuit, thus ending what is commonly called the "Burlington Races."

The most significant loss on Lake Ontario in 1813 was caused not by a battle but by Mother Nature. The United States had a pair of converted merchantmen on the lake, the *Hamilton* (9 guns) and the *Scourge* (10 guns). Both were top heavy because of the naval guns they carried. According to Ned Myers, one of the *Scourge's* crewmen, his ship was "unfit for her duty," and it was often said that "she would prove our coffin." For many of Myers's shipmates, this proved to be correct, for both vessels sank after capsizing in a storm in the early morning hours of August 8. All but sixteen of the one hundred men aboard perished. (These vessels have since been found—perfectly preserved in 300 feet of water—near Hamilton, Ontario.)

The Battle of York

Although Chauncey and Yeo avoided naval engagements, each was willing to support amphibious operations, especially if the target was an enemy naval base. American strategy called for assaulting the main British naval base at Kingston, but Chauncey and Dearborn decided to substitute the secondary naval base at York (present-day

Toronto) because it was an easier target. Chauncey ferried a U.S. force of 2,600 soldiers, seamen, and marines from Sackets Harbor to York, arriving on April 27. York, then the provincial capital of Upper Canada, was defended by around 1,000 troops and fifty to one hundred Indians under the command of Major General Roger Sheaffe.

Although Dearborn had command of the American force, characteristically he remained on Chauncey's flagship, while Brigadier General Zebulon Pike commanded the landing force, which was spearheaded by American rifle units. Aided by supporting fire from Chauncey's squadron, the invaders drove off the Indians who had contested the landing and then forced Sheaffe to withdraw from York to the east.

Before departing, the British set a fuse to blow up the main powder magazine. The ensuing explosion was tremendous, rattling windows at Fort Niagara more than thirty miles away and causing extensive injuries to the approaching American troops. Among the casualties was Brigadier General Pike, who was killed when "a large stone struck him in the forehead and stamped him for the grave." In all, the American assault force sustained 310 casualties, most caused by the explosion, while the British suffered only 200 killed and wounded and another 275 captured.

Angry over the explosion, American soldiers looted the town. They were joined by many locals who had come in from the countryside. "Every house they found deserted was completely sacked," complained one resident. The Americans also burned the government buildings. Dearborn, who had come ashore, was slow to end the lawlessness because he was convinced that the navy yard and a ship there had been put to the torch after city officials had begun negotiations for surrender. He restored order only after local clergyman John Strachan (who later became the first Anglican bishop of Toronto) shamed him into action. The burning of York was the first of a series of such incidents that prompted the British to retaliate when they occupied the U.S. capital the following year.

The Assault on Fort George

The attack on York was but a prelude to a more ambitious operation at the western end of Lake Ontario that targeted Fort George, a British post at the mouth of the Niagara River that was defended by 1,500 British regulars, militia, and Indians under the command of Brigadier General John Vincent. After assembling some 4,000 men at Fort Niagara, the Americans pounded the British side of the river for two days with artillery fire. Then on May 27, Chauncey ferried the army to the back side of Fort George and laid an artillery barrage to cover the landing, a joint operation managed by Colonel Winfield Scott and Master Commandant Oliver H. Perry (who had not yet won his laurels on Lake Erie).

The British came out to meet the invaders, but outgunned and outmanned they soon had to retreat, abandoning not only Fort George but the rest of their positions on the west bank of the Niagara River all the way up to Fort Erie. Scott was eager to pursue the British but was ordered back by a timid New York militia major general who was in command of all the American land forces. The British lost 350 men in the battle, the United States 140. But without the pursuit, Vincent was able to regroup at Burlington Heights (now Hamilton) with about 1,600 men.

American Setbacks

When Major General Henry Dearborn, who had overall command on the Niagara, ordered 2,500 men under two brigadiers, John Chandler and William Winder, to challenge the British at Burlington Heights, they were surprised by 750 men led by Lieutenant Colonel John Harvey at Stoney Creek on June 5–6, 1813, in a night attack. The Americans retreated when their artillery batteries were overrun, and in the confusion both American generals blundered into British units and were captured. Although the United States sustained only 170 casualties compared to 215 for the British, they fled without burying their dead or taking all their equipment.

After the debacle at Stoney Creek, Dearborn concentrated all of his forces on the Canadian side of the Niagara River at Fort George. The British responded by establishing a series of outposts nearby so that they could harass anyone who ventured from the post. In late June Lieutenant Colonel Charles Boerstler led 600 men from the fort to mount a surprise attack on a British outpost that was garrisoned by fifty men under Lieutenant James FitzGibbon.

FitzGibbon was warned of the attack by Indians as well as by a Canadian woman, Laura Secord, who walked twenty miles through rough and unfamiliar territory at night. But on June 24, before Boerstler got to the British outpost, he was ambushed at Beaver Dams by a large Indian party led by Captain Dominique Ducharme of the Indian Department. FitzGibbon then appeared and convinced Boerstler to surrender to the large British force that he claimed to have with him. This defeat was the last straw for Dearborn's critics, who persuaded the president to transfer him to a non-combat zone.

For the rest of the summer and fall, the British and their Indian allies held the initiative on the Niagara and maintained a loose siege of Fort George. The ranks of the American troops at the fort thinned as units were transferred east to take part in a major campaign against Montreal. Brigadier General George McClure of the New York militia, who was in command at Fort George, was unable to raise volunteer militia to replace the departing regulars.

With his force steadily shrinking, McClure concluded that he could no longer hold the fort and on December 10 ordered it abandoned. Before leaving, he ordered the nearby village of Newark put to the torch. The inhabitants were given only a few hours' notice before being forced into the cold winter weather. "Every building in

Newark is reduced to ashes," McClure reported; "the enemy is much exasperated and will make a descent on this frontier if possible."

British Retaliation

McClure's prediction was on the mark. Lieutenant General Gordon Drummond, who now had command of all of the British forces on the Niagara, was furious over the burning of Newark. After the British had reoccupied Fort George, Drummond dispatched 550 men under Colonel John Murray across the river for a night attack on Fort Niagara. On December 19, after surprising a sentry and securing the password, Murray's men burst into the fort and fell upon the sleeping Americans. "Our men," reported McClure, "were nearly all asleep in their tents; the enemy rushed in and commenced a most horrid slaughter." The British inflicted 80 casualties, mainly with their bayonets, and took 350 prisoners while sustaining only a dozen casualties. They also acquired a huge cache of war material.

After securing Fort Niagara, the British sent a force under Major General Phineas Riall (pronounced Rile) to torch Lewiston and other nearby towns. Riall returned on December 30 to attack Black Rock and Buffalo. After routing the defenders, the British looted and burned both towns. A campaign that had such a promising start in May with the capture of Fort George had by December ended in disaster with the British in control of both forts at the mouth of the Niagara River and the American side of the river in flames. "The whole frontier from Lake Ontario to Lake Erie," lamented the governor of New York, "is depopulated and the buildings and Improvements, with a few exceptions, destroyed."

The Battle of Sackets Harbor

At the eastern end of Lake Ontario, the campaign of 1813 also had a promising start for the United States. On May 29, while Chauncey was at the other end of the lake taking part in the assault on Fort George, the British launched their own amphibious attack against Sackets Harbor and the crucial naval base there. The assault force, about 1,000 strong, was under the command of Colonel Edward Baynes (although his superior, Governor Prevost, was also aboard). The American base was defended by 1,450 regulars and militia under the command of Brigadier General Jacob Brown of the New York militia.

Brown's militiamen were unable to hold their ground, but the U.S. regulars and a 32-pounder at Fort Tompkins took a heavy toll on the British assault force. When an American midshipman mistakenly concluded that the battle was lost, he set fire to the navy yard. Although a hastily organized fire brigade put the fire out, the smoke convinced Baynes that the navy yard was destroyed, and (with Prevost's blessing) he ordered a withdrawal. The British had suffered 260 casualties, the Americans only 155, although another 140 were captured. For the successful defense of Sackets Harbor, Brown was commissioned a brigadier general in the U.S. Army and made a name for himself on the Niagara frontier the following year.

Montreal Targeted

Although Montreal was not at first on the War Department's target list in 1813, it was added in July, and the result was the largest U.S. offensive in the war. The plan was for Major General James Wilkinson to lead one army from Sackets Harbor down the St. Lawrence River to approach Montreal from the west, while a second army under the command of Major General Wade Hampton would approach from Plattsburgh in the south. From the beginning, however, this double-barreled operation was beset by problems. It was undertaken late in the season when bad weather threatened, and neither commander had much confidence in the campaign or showed the kind of leadership needed to make it a success. Wilkinson was a longtime Spanish spy who pursued his own interest at the expense of all else, while Hampton was a haughty South Carolina planter who so despised Wilkinson that he refused to take orders from him.

In mid-September, Hampton moved an army, 6,000 strong, to the north end of Lake Champlain and after crossing the border fought his way into Odelltown. He then veered to the west and headed north along the Châteauguay River. Blocking his path were over 1,800 troops, mostly French Canadian quasi-regular and militia units, plus 150 Indians, all under the command of Lieutenant Colonel Charles de Salaberry. Although most of Hampton's militia stayed behind, he still had 3,800 men. Despite his numerical superiority, in the battle that ensued on October 26, Hampton could not break through enemy lines even though he launched offensives on both sides of the river. Casualties on both sides in the Battle of Châteauguay were light—less than a hundred combined—but Hampton concluded that the operation could not succeed and ordered his men back to Plattsburgh.

Wilkinson was no more successful with his operation. Although he had a huge army, 7,300 strong, he did not make it from Sackets Harbor to the mouth of the St. Lawrence until early November. As he moved his force downriver, he had to contend with harassment from the northern shore and with a trailing British force of 1,200 soldiers and Indians under the command of thirty-year-old Lieutenant Colonel Joseph W. Morrison. When Morrison took up a position on the north shore at Crysler's Farm, Wilkinson on November 11 dispatched forty-eight-year-old Brigadier General John P. Boyd and 3,000 men to dislodge him. But Boyd sent his men into battle piecemeal and without enough ammunition and thus his force got hammered, forcing him to order a retreat. In the Battle of Crysler's Farm, the United States had sustained about

400 casualties and the British about half this number. With this defeat, Wilkinson called off the campaign and went into winter quarters.

Genesis of the Creek War

The United States waged a war against the Creeks in the Old Southwest in 1813, but unlike in the Old Northwest the Indians fought without any help from the British. The Creeks occupied much of Alabama and Georgia, and at the urging of the American Indian agent, many, especially the mixed-bloods, had embraced the white man's civilization. Although they still hunted, they also practiced agriculture, raised livestock, recognized private property, and even adopted slavery. But a band of Creeks rejected assimilation and nursed a host of grievances against the white man. Known as "Red Sticks" because they carried red war clubs, they were eager to return to their traditional ways and to roll back the ever-advancing American frontier.

Tecumseh had visited the Creeks in 1811, hoping to persuade them to join his confederation and his crusade against whites. The Red Sticks were receptive, and some traveled north and took part in the Battle of Frenchtown and the River Raisin Massacre in 1813. On the way home, they killed some settlers in Kentucky. To keep peace with the United States, the old Creek chiefs ordered the guilty Indians hunted down and killed. This led to a civil war between Creek factions, forcing the old chiefs to seek refuge with the American agent. With the Red Sticks in the ascendant, depredations against American settlements in the Old Southwest increased.

In the summer of 1813 a group of Red Sticks visited Pensacola to trade for European goods and pick up arms promised by Spanish officials. On July 27, as they were returning home, they were ambushed by 180 militiamen led by Colonel James Caller about eighty miles north of Pensacola. In the Battle of Burnt Corn, the Americans got away with most of the Indian pack animals, but the ease with which a much smaller band of Indians drove them off emboldened the Red Sticks. This battle transformed the civil war within the Creek Confederacy into America's Creek War.

The Red Sticks retaliated by targeting Fort Mims, a stockade about forty miles north of Mobile that housed about 300 people, including 120 militia under the command of Major Daniel Beasley, a regular army officer. Beasley did not expect an attack, and he ignored reports that Indians were seen lurking nearby. Hence, he was unprepared when the attack came on August 30. Led by William Weatherford, a Scottish-Cherokee leader also known as Red Eagle, the Red Sticks overran the fort. Although the Creeks paid dearly, losing at least one hundred killed and many more wounded, they killed some 250 Americans, including women and children. The only survivors were a few Americans who escaped into the wilderness and some black slaves who were carried off by the victors.

Early reports exaggerated the number of Americans killed and "spread consternation through the territory." The Fort Mims Massacre galvanized people in the Old Southwest much as the River Raisin Massacre had in the Old Northwest. There were widespread demands for retaliation, and people in Georgia and the Mississippi Territory were quick to answer the call. Volunteers were recruited and militia drafted for guard duty and punitive expeditions.

Most impressive was the prowess shown by Captain Sam Dale, known as "Big Sam" to the Indians, who had been wounded at Burnt Corn. By November Dale had recovered enough to lead forty men up the Alabama River in search of predatory Indians. Reaching what is today Monroe County, Alabama, Dale took part on November 12 in a legendary skirmish known as the "Canoe Fight." Boarding a large Indian dugout, Dale killed several Indians in hand-to-hand combat. His feat gave people in the territory both a victory to celebrate and a hero to honor. Other expeditions from Georgia and the Mississippi Territory took a toll on the Red Sticks, but the results were far from conclusive.

Jackson's Campaign

People in Tennessee also responded to the call. In the fall of 1813 some 2,500 militia and volunteers were recruited for a punitive expedition. The troops included Davy Crockett, who reportedly kept "the camp alive with his quaint conceits and marvelous narratives." Andrew Jackson, a major general in the Tennessee militia, assumed command of the troops even though he was still recovering from bullet wounds suffered in a brawl with the Benton brothers, Jesse and Thomas Hart. A tough Indian fighter who was already known as "Old Hickory," Jackson planned to wipe out the Red Sticks.

Jackson defeated the Red Sticks at Tallushatchee on November 3 and at Talladega on November 9. But after that he faced a growing number of challenges: undisciplined troops, expiring enlistments, and recurring supply shortages. At times he could only keep his army together only by threatening to fire on men who planned to return home. In January 1814 Jackson won a pair of additional victories, first at Emuckfau and then at Enotachopco Creek. Eventually, word of his success attracted more volunteers, and he was also given 600 regulars. By February Jackson's army was 6,000 strong.

On March 27 Jackson targeted the main Red Stick camp, a fortified village on a peninsula known as Horseshoe Bend on the Tallapoosa River deep in Creek country. While Jackson pounded the Indian breastworks with two small field pieces, friendly Indians swam across the river and made off with canoes that the Red Sticks had placed on the shore in case they had to escape. The artillery bombardment was ineffective, so Jackson ordered a frontal assault. At the same time, the Red Stick camp was assailed from the rear by troops and friendly Indians who crossed the river.

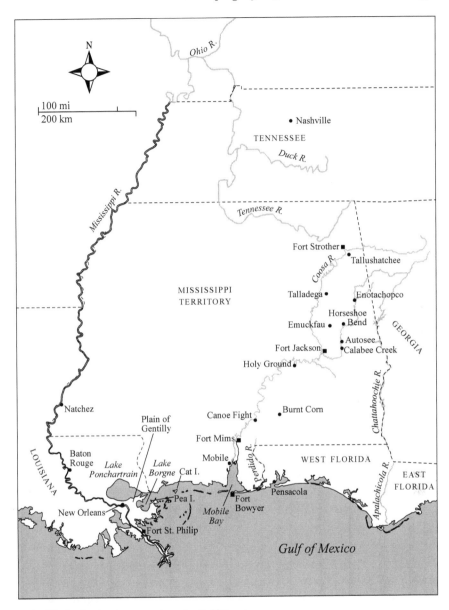

The War in the Southwest and on the Gulf Coast

Once the Red Stick defenses were breached, a disorganized battle raged, continuing into the night. The Battle of Horseshoe Bend was a slaughter. No quarter was asked, and none was given. The *"carnage,"* Jackson told his wife, "was *dreadful."* The Red Sticks sustained 800 deaths, while Jackson's own casualties were only 200 killed and wounded.

After Horseshoe Bend, some of surviving Red Sticks fled to Florida, where they joined the Seminoles. Others, including William Weatherford, surrendered. Weatherford helped persuade other Red Sticks to make peace and rebuilt his life and ended his days as an affluent Alabama planter. Jackson forced all Creek leaders, friend and foe alike, to sign the Treaty of Fort Jackson on August 9. This draconian agreement stripped the Creeks of 36,000 square miles of land, which was over half of their territory. The Treaty of Fort Jackson raised eyebrows in the nation's capital but was applauded by westerners.

Jackson's triumph in the Old Southwest, like those of Perry and Harrison in the Old Northwest, increased American security and paved the way for western expansion. The only problem with these victories is that they occurred in regions that were too remote to affect the outcome of the war with Great Britain. On the more important fronts—along the Niagara and St. Lawrence rivers—the United States had encountered only failure. After two years of campaigning, Canada remained in British hands, and victory for the United States seemed as elusive as ever.

The British Blockade

If the war on land went better for the United States in 1813, the war at sea went worse. This was to be expected because the ocean was Britain's element. The British had been slow to exploit their naval superiority in the first six months of the war, which had led to considerable domestic criticism. In response, the Admiralty increased its naval strength in American waters to ten ships-of-the-line, thirty-eight frigates, and fifty-two smaller vessels.

The Admiralty also lectured Admiral Sir John Borlase Warren, who was put in charge of all British naval forces in the North Atlantic and Caribbean, on what was expected of him in the ensuing campaign. "It is of the highest importance to the *character* and interests of the country," wrote the Admiralty, "that the naval force of the enemy should be quickly and completely disposed of." Warren was "to bring the naval war to a termination, either by the capture of the American national vessels, or by strictly blockading them in their own waters."

Warren had already established an informal blockade from Charleston, South Carolina, to Spanish Florida in the fall of 1812. He extended this blockade in December to the Chesapeake and Delaware bays, and, when his fleet was enlarged in 1813, to other ports and harbors in the middle and southern states. Thus by November 1813 the entire coast south of New England was under blockade. Warren exempted New England, both to reward it for its opposition to the war and to keep up the flow of provisions from that region to Canada and the British West Indies.

The British blockade had a crushing impact on American foreign trade. "Commerce is becoming very slack," reported a resident of Baltimore in the spring of 1813;

"no arrivals from abroad, & nothing going to sea but sharp [that is, fast] vessels." By the end of the year, the sea lanes had become so dangerous that merchants wishing to insure oceangoing voyages had to shell out 50 percent of the value of the ship and cargo.

With British warships hovering nearby, the coasting trade had become perilous, too, forcing American merchants to resort to overland transportation. But there were few good roads, and even the best broke down under heavy use and the ongoing assault of the elements. "The roads [in Virginia] . . . are worse than usual," Nathaniel Macon reported in March 1813; "it takes 38 hours to travel from Fredericksburg to Alexandria, the distance 50 miles."

The reduction in trade created gluts and shortages everywhere. Sugar that sold for $9 a hundredweight in August 1813 in New Orleans commanded $21.50 in New York and $26.50 in Baltimore. Rice selling for $3 a hundredweight in Charleston or Savannah brought $9 in New York and $12 in Philadelphia. Flour, which was $4.50 a barrel in Richmond, fetched $8.50 in New York and almost $12 in Boston.

The U.S. Treasury also felt the impact of the blockade because tax revenue was heavily dependent on foreign trade. Although the taxes on trade had been doubled at the beginning of the war, government income, which stood at $14 million in 1811, declined to $10 million in 1812 and rose only back to $14 million in 1813. With the cost of the war driving up government expenditures, the administration found itself increasingly strapped for money and increasingly dependent on public loans.

British Raids in the Chesapeake

The British used their naval power in another way, conducting numerous raids on the coast, mainly in the Chesapeake Bay. Their aim was twofold: to try to draw American troops away from the Canadian frontier and to bring the war home to Americans. Warren, who had no stomach for raiding and plundering, assigned the command in these waters to Rear Admiral Sir George Cockburn (pronounced Coburn). Cockburn was a bold and able officer in the prime of a long and distinguished naval career. Guided through the countryside by runaway slaves, he supervised many of the raids in the Chesapeake.

In the spring of 1813, the British targeted the north end of the Chesapeake Bay, burning Frenchtown, Havre de Grace, Georgetown, and Fredericktown, Maryland. They also destroyed an important cannon foundry at Principio. The only time they were rebuffed was at Fort Defiance, which spared the town of Elkton. Otherwise, they moved freely on American soil for two weeks without meeting effective resistance.

On June 22, Colonel Thomas Sidney Beckwith and Captain Samuel J. Pechell of the Royal Navy led some 2,400 men by land and water against Norfolk, Virginia, a regional commercial center that harbored the frigate *Constellation*. Brigadier General

Robert B. Taylor of the Virginia militia offered effective artillery resistance, and both wings of the British attack had to withdraw when they ran into natural obstacles. In the Battle of Craney Island, the British lost eighty men, the Americans none.

Three days later the British attacked Hampton, Virginia. The militia put up surprisingly stout resistance before being overwhelmed and forced to retreat. After the fighting ended, two independent companies of foreigners consisting of French prisoners of war and deserters committed a host of atrocities on the civilian population. According to Lieutenant Colonel Charles Napier, a young British officer who later gained fame in India, "every horror was committed with impunity, rape, murder, pillage: and not a man was punished!" The French units were dispatched to Halifax, where they remained unruly until they were finally sent back to Europe and disbanded.

The British occupied Kent Island in early August and renewed their raids on the Eastern Shore, but this time with less success. They suffered heavy casualties in an attack at Queenstown on August 13, in part because in the confusion they fired on one another. The British also targeted St. Michaels, first on August 10 and then again on August 26, but unaccountably withdrew without destroying the town's shipyard. A story surfaced in the late nineteenth century that residents induced the British to overshoot the mark with their artillery in the first attack by hanging lanterns in trees and two-story houses, but there is no contemporary evidence to support this tale.

The British depredations caused a great deal of bitterness in the Chesapeake. *Niles' Register* attacked Warren and dubbed his troops "water-*Winnebagoes*"—an allusion to the most militant Indians in the Old Northwest. Cockburn drew even greater fire. "The wantonness of his barbarities," said *Niles,* "have gibbetted him on infamy." Some Americans, however, benefited from the British presence. When they met with no resistance, the British usually paid for the provisions they needed. Those willing to do business with the invaders—and there were many—profited handsomely. In addition, a growing number of runaway slaves found sanctuary with the British. For them the British presence in the Chesapeake meant a new start in life as freedmen.

Naval Engagements

There were fewer naval engagements in 1813 than in 1812 because most U.S. warships were bottled up in port. Even those that managed to slip out to sea found the pickings slim because British warships sailed in squadrons and British merchantmen in convoy. The Navy Department ordered American warships to cruise separately and to avoid combat except under the most favorable circumstances. Nevertheless, there were three naval engagements, and two ended in defeat for the United States.

The lone victory belonged to the American brig *Enterprise* (16 guns), which on September 5 found the British sloop *Boxer* (14 guns) off the coast of Maine. The two ships slugged it out for over an hour before the British vessel struck its colors. Both commanding officers were killed in the engagement. In another engagement, which took place on August 14, the British sloop *Pelican* (21 guns) defeated the U.S. brig *Argus* (20 guns) off the coast of Ireland. After this loss, the War Department ordered its smaller warships to concentrate on commerce destruction.

Defeat of the *Chesapeake*

The British also enjoyed their first victory over an American frigate in 1813. In May of that year thirty-one-year-old Captain James Lawrence, who had earlier commanded the U.S. sloop *Hornet* (20 guns) in its victory over the British sloop *Peacock* (20 guns), was given command of the *Chesapeake* (50 guns). The American frigate was fitted out in Boston. With inexperienced officers and a crew in need of training, *Chesapeake* desperately needed a shakedown cruise. But Lawrence was eager to do battle and ignored this.

Hovering off the coast of Boston were two British frigates, the *Shannon* (52 guns), commanded by thirty-five-year-old Captain Philip Broke (pronounced Brook), and the *Tenedos* (47 guns?). Broke was a superb officer who had been cruising in the *Shannon* since 1806. Using his own money, he outfitted his ship with special aiming devices, and, unlike other British naval commanders after Trafalgar, he drilled his crew incessantly in gunnery using live ammunition. According to a British officer who was assigned to the American station, "The *Shannon's* men were better trained, and understood gunnery better, than any men I ever saw."

As the *Chesapeake* was preparing to sail, Broke sent the *Tenedos* away and dispatched a challenge to Lawrence for a meeting "Ship to Ship, to try the fortunes of our respective Flags." Lawrence sailed before this challenge arrived, but he needed no invitation. On June 1 the *Chesapeake* emerged from port flying a banner that read "Free Trade and Sailors Rights." Lawrence made for the *Shannon* but unaccountably passed up a chance to rake the British ship. Instead, the two ships lined up parallel to each other and exchanged broadsides at close range.

Superior gunnery quickly carried the day for the *Shannon*, taking a terrific toll on the American officers, men, and ship. The *Chesapeake* lost control, was subjected to a murderous raking fire, and then boarded. Lawrence was wounded but repeatedly urged his men to fight on, uttering "Don't give up the ship" and similar expressions. His men, however, suffered heavy casualties and had no choice but to surrender. Lawrence's wounds were mortal, but he lingered on for three days after the battle and thus knew the fate of his ship. The British took control of the *Chesapeake* and sailed her into Halifax as a prize of war.

The *Shannon's* victory, which was accomplished quickly over a ship of equal firepower, gave a huge boost to the British morale. The news was greeted in Parliament with the "loudest and most cordial acclamations from every part of the House."

This idealized picture shows the death of Captain James Lawrence of U.S. frigate *Chesapeake*. (J. A. Spencer, *History of the United States*)

After a long string of defeats, the victory restored the reputation of the Royal Navy. Although Broke never fully recovered from a head wound received in the battle, he was made a baronet and showered with gifts from an appreciative nation.

Lawrence, on the other hand, received a hero's funeral in New York City that was reportedly attended by 50,000 people. The Navy Department named Perry's flagship on Lake Erie after Lawrence, and Perry immortalized Lawrence's words—"Don't give up the ship"—by putting them on his battle flag. After Perry's great victory on Lake Erie, the phrase became the motto of the U.S. Navy and replaced "Free Trade and Sailors' Rights" as the rallying cry of the war.

American Privateering

With most of the nation's warships bottled up in port by the British blockade, privateers had to shoulder a heavier share of the war at sea, although pickings were slim because the British had adopted the convoy system. To find prizes, privateers had to cruise in the British West Indies or near the British Isles, for it was only in those waters that the British government did not require merchantmen to sail in convoy.

The most spectacular cruise was made by the *True-Blooded Yankee* (16 guns), a small vessel fitted out by an American citizen in Paris. On a thirty-seven-day cruise in waters around the British Isles, this ship took twenty-seven prizes, occupied an Irish island for six days, and burned seven vessels in a Scottish harbor. "She outsailed everything," marveled a British naval officer; "not one of our cruisers could touch her." The *Scourge* (15 guns) and *Rattlesnake* (16 guns) found equally good hunting in the North Sea. Between them they took twenty-three prizes, which were sent into Norwegian ports for condemnation. The *Scourge* made another successful cruise and then took additional prizes on her way home.

End of the Campaign

The outcome of the campaign of 1813 should have occasioned no surprise because the American victories on land and the British victories at sea accorded with the general strengths of the two nations. Although Americans could be justly proud of their triumphs, final victory continued to elude them, and now, more than ever, time was running against them.

In October 1813 Great Britain's allies had defeated Napoleon in the decisive Battle of Leipzig. Coupled with the British triumphs in Spain, this foreshadowed Napoleon's downfall. With these victories behind them, the British began diverting men and material to the New World, and this changed the whole complexion of the American war. Having failed to conquer Canada in 1812 or 1813, the United States would not get another chance. When the campaign of 1814 opened, the British were in the driver's seat.

Chapter 4

The British Counteroffensive, 1814–1815

By the time the campaigning season opened in 1814, the initiative in the war had shifted to the British. The Battle of Leipzig the previous October had forced Napoleon to retreat to France, with the Allies in pursuit. On March 31, the Allies entered Paris. Napoleon abdicated unconditionally on April 11 and shortly thereafter was exiled to the Mediterranean island of Elba. For the first time in more than a decade, Europe was at peace.

Federalists celebrated the defeat of Napoleon, and some Republicans joined them. "I rejoice with you," Jefferson told a friend, "in the downfall of Bonaparte. This scourge of the world has occasioned the deaths of at least ten millions of human beings."

The Changing Character of the War

The problem with France's defeat was that it left the United States alone in the field against Great Britain, and most Republicans expected the British to be vindictive. "We should have to fight hereafter," predicted Joseph Nicholson of Maryland, "not for 'free trade and sailors' rights,' not for the conquest of the Canadas, but for our national existence." As the character of the war changed, so, too, did the nation's motto. "Don't give up the ship" gave way to "Don't give up the soil."

Ever since Leipzig, the British had been cautiously shifting troops from Europe to North America, and with Napoleon's defeat, the pace of this redeployment picked up. By September 1814 the British had 30,000 troops in the American war, and by the end of the year the number had soared to 52,000.

Fortunately for the United States, the American army was steadily improving. The men in the ranks were better trained, and many now had significant combat experience. Moreover, two years of campaigning had weeded out many incompetent officers, and Secretary of War John Armstrong, who was a fair judge of talent, was advancing capable young men up the command ladder. The generous enlistment bounty also began to tell. By the spring of 1814, the army was 40,000 strong, and by early 1815 its strength had climbed to almost 45,000.

When the campaigning season opened in 1814, the British were able to take the offensive, but only in the East near their sources of supply. Further west, the United States enjoyed the advantage of shorter and more secure supply lines, which meant that it could remain on the offensive. As a result, the United States remained in the ascendant in the Old Northwest, and even on the Niagara front it challenged the British for control.

Trading Blows in the West

In the Old Northwest, the United States targeted the two remaining British strong-holds. A small Anglo-Indian force held Prairie du Chien, which was strategically located near the confluence of the Mississippi and Wisconsin rivers, and a much larger Anglo-Indian force controlled Mackinac Island, which dominated the upper lakes. In June an American force headed by the governor of the Missouri Territory, William Clark (of Lewis and Clark fame), seized Prairie du Chien, but the British retook the village in July and held it for the rest of the war.

The British also beat back an assault on Fort Mackinac on August 4, and in a further blow to American power on the upper lakes captured two U.S. schooners, the *Tigress* (1 gun) and the *Scorpion* (2 guns), in early September. The British retained Mackinac until the war was over, which enabled them to supply, and thus retain the loyalty of, those Indians who had not defected to the United States after the Battle of the Thames. As a result, Indian raids continued to menace the western frontier despite American dominance in the region.

Even though the British retained Prairie du Chien and Mackinac, they could not protect their subjects in western Upper Canada, and American raiding parties from Detroit operated against these settlements with impunity. One American raiding party under Colonel John B. Campbell burned Dover and other nearby settlements on the north shore of Lake Erie in May, which contributed to the British decision to burn the public buildings in Washington in August. Another U.S. force, mounted and led by Brigadier General Duncan McArthur, conducted a deep raid into Up-per Canada in November, burning mills that were loaded with the fall harvest as far east as the Grand River and defeating a militia force in the Battle of Malcolm's Mills on November 6. Furious over the McArthur's destruction of private property, Governor George Prevost ordered retaliation, but the war ended before his order could be carried out.

Bloody Slugfest on the Niagara

The United States launched its biggest offensive in 1814 on the Niagara front, and the result was the bloodiest fighting of the entire war. Major General Jacob Brown (the hero of Sackets Harbor) was now in command of all the American forces in this theater, some 5,500 men. He was assisted by Brigadier General Winfield Scott, who had trained a crack brigade the previous spring; by one-time congressional War Hawk Peter B. Porter, a militia brigadier who headed New York and Pennsylvania units that took part in the campaign; by Lieutenant Colonel Joseph Willcocks, who commanded a group of defectors known as the Canadian Volunteers; and by the aging Seneca chief Red Jacket, who brought some 500 Iroquois into the field.

Opposing the Americans was a British force about 4,000 strong under the command of Major General Phineas Riall, who also could count on 500 Grand River Iroquois led by Mohawk chief John Norton. At stake in the heavy fighting that ensued was control of the Niagara Peninsula.

On July 3, Brown moved his army across the Niagara River and besieged Fort Erie, which surrendered after offering only token resistance. Brown ordered Scott to lead his brigade north along the river road. The clash that ensued on July 5 pitted an American and Indian force of about 2,000 men against a British and Indian force of roughly the same strength. American artillery pounded the British, while Scott's men, who were dressed in gray uniforms because blue cloth was unavailable, coolly maneuvered despite heavy enemy artillery fire. Convinced that the gray uniforms signified militia, Riall was surprised at the discipline he saw and reportedly exclaimed, "Why, those are regulars!" thus contributing to U.S. Army lore.

Riall's troops advanced within musket range but got the worst of several volleys exchanged with Scott's men. An American advance forced the right side of the British line to sag, and Riall ordered a retreat across the Chippawa River. In the Battle of Chippawa, the United States lost 325 killed, wounded, and missing; the British about 500. The American victory, the first against a British force of equal strength in the war, was a tribute to the long hours of training by Scott's men. Since the cadets at West Point wore gray uniforms, the Military Academy later embraced the notion that its uniforms honored the performance of the U.S. Army on the Niagara frontier in 1814.

By late July Lieutenant General Gordon Drummond had arrived on the front with British reinforcements and took command from Riall. Determined to drive the Americans from the Niagara Peninsula, Drummond ordered 1,600 men to take up a position on a ridge that was near Lundy's Lane and within earshot of the roar of Niagara Falls. On July 25 Scott, always aggressive, attacked with about 1,200 men, and soon both sides were reinforced until about 3,000 men were engaged on each side.

Scott's brigade was shredded by British artillery fire and by his reckless march across the battlefield. Saving the day for the Americans was Colonel James Miller, whose regiment overran the British artillery batteries with a bayonet charge launched after a musket volley. Drummond repeatedly counterattacked but could not retake the guns. The battle finally ended when Brown ordered a withdrawal. By this time both sides were too exhausted to fight anymore.

Colonel Miller described the six-hour Battle of Lundy's Lane as "one of the most desperately fought actions ever experienced in America," which was probably true. All four senior officers—Brown, Scott, Drummond, and Riall—were wounded. Scott was knocked out of the war, and Riall was captured. The Americans sustained fewer casualties—860 to 880 for the British—but suffered twice as many deaths from the deadly British artillery fire. The battle was essentially a draw.

After Lundy's Lane, the Americans, about 2,200 strong, withdrew to Fort Erie, which had been greatly expanded and strengthened. Brigadier General Edmund P. Gaines took command and, anticipating a British assault, made sure that his men were ready. His vigilance paid off.

For two days, starting on August 13, Lieutenant General Drummond softened up Fort Erie with artillery fire. Then in the early morning hours of August 15, he launched a risky night attack that ended in disaster for the British. An Indian demonstration planned for the west side of the fort never materialized. Attacking the south end of the fort was a force of 1,300 men under the command of Lieutenant Colonel Victor Fischer. The troops had been ordered to remove their flints to ensure surprise, which meant they could not respond when they reached the fort

This illustration shows Colonel James Miller's storming of British batteries in the Battle of Lundy's Lane. (Robert Tomes, *Battles of America by Land and Sea*)

and were fired on. Since their ladders were too short to reach the top of the fort's breastworks, they had little choice but to withdraw.

Two other British assault forces targeted the north end of the fort with about 1,000 men. Both the commanding officers, Colonel Hercules Scott and Lieutenant Colonel William Drummond (General Drummond's nephew), were killed, but the British penetrated a bastion and engaged in close combat for about a half hour before a powder magazine accidentally exploded, blowing up virtually the entire British force and thus ending the battle. "The explosion," reported Gaines, "was tremendous—it was decisive." The British lost over 900 men, most of whom were killed, while American casualties were only eighty-five. As the casualty figures suggest, the Battle of Fort Erie was a clear American victory.

In the ensuing month, the opposing forces exchanged artillery fire. Gaines was seriously wounded, forcing Major General Brown to resume command even though he had not yet recovered from wounds received at Lundy's Lane. When the British began mounting guns within 500 yards of the fort, Brown's officers urged an evacuation. But Brigadier General Peter B. Porter arrived with some 2,000 militia, and Brown decided to try to storm the British batteries first.

In a driving rainstorm on the night of September 17, 1,200 New York militia under Porter and 800 regulars under Lieutenant Colonel Miller surprised the British batteries. After heavy fighting, they overran two of the batteries and spiked the guns before being forced to retreat. In what is known as the Sortie from Fort Erie, the Americans lost 510 men, the British 720. One American officer thought this was "the most splendid achievement" of the campaign, and Brown was particularly happy with the performance of the New York militia. "They have behaved gallantly," he commented.

Even before the U.S. sortie, Drummond had decided to pull back to the north side of the Chippawa River. His men were running low on food and ammunition, and the incessant rains that summer left everyone wet and prone to disease.

In early October Major General George Izard arrived at Fort Erie with additional men and superseded Brown in command. Eager to engage the British, Izard marched north along the river road, but he found that Drummond was in a strong position north of the Chippawa River and refused to be drawn out. There was minor engagement at Cook's Mills on October 19 when an American detachment under Brigadier General Daniel Bissell was sent to seize or destroy some grain and had to drive off a British force to achieve its mission. This was the last action of the campaign.

Because Fort Erie continued to be difficult to supply, the Americans blew it up on November 5 and returned to New York. The campaign on the Niagara front in 1814 was the bloodiest of the war, accounting for more than 25 percent of all combat casualties. The fighting had boosted the reputation of the U.S. Army by showing that it could hold its own against British veterans. But otherwise the results of the campaign were meager. Brown's offensive had been blunted, and the British retained control of the Niagara Peninsula.

Oswego and Sandy Creek

The British were able to compete more effectively on Lake Ontario than Lake Erie because their sources of supply were closer. By October the British had won control of Lake Ontario by putting into service the *St. Lawrence,* a 104-gun ship-of-the-line that had more firepower than any other ship in the Royal Navy. The United States countered by building its own ships-of-the-line, but the war ended before they were finished.

Even before the *St. Lawrence* was ready for action, Commodore James Yeo had been able to take advantage of temporary superiority on the lake to make an assault on Oswego. This village was an important way station in the American supply line that ran from New York City to the naval base at Sackets Harbor. Supplies were transported north on the Hudson River to Albany and then west along the Mohawk River and other waterways to Oswego on Lake Ontario. From there they were moved by water along the shoreline to Sackets Harbor.

In early May Commodore Yeo ferried 900 men under Lieutenant General Drummond to Oswego, which was protected by a decrepit post named Fort Ontario that was garrisoned by 300 men under Lieutenant Colonel George E. Mitchell. On May 6 the British landed, defeated the Americans who met them on the shore, and then overran the fort. The British destroyed the fort and withdrew with some food and war material. Fortunately for the United States, they were unaware of a large cache of naval guns and rope intended for Sackets Harbor that had been stashed twelve miles above the fort at Oswego Falls (present-day Fulton, New York).

After the British left, the Americans moved the naval guns and rope to Oswego and then loaded them onto a flotilla of gunboats commanded by Master Commandant Melancthon Woolsey for shipment to Sackets Harbor. With a British squadron nearby, Woolsey traveled at night and hugged the shoreline, taking refuge in Sandy Creek on May 30. To protect the valuable cargo, 300 men from Sackets Harbor arrived along with 120 Oneida Indians.

Captain Stephen Popham, who was on detached duty from the British squadron, discovered Woolsey's presence in the creek and led a flotilla of gunboats carrying 200 men upriver to mount an attack. The British got mauled by the Americans on the shore, and the survivors surrendered. Since it was too dangerous to return to the lake, the guns and rope were moved overland to Sackets Harbor about twenty miles away.

There was, however, one rope that was 300 feet long and seven inches in diameter and weighed nearly five tons. Since no wagon was big enough to transport it, Colonel Allen Clark's regiment of New York militia offered to carry the rope.

Part of the rope was loaded into the largest wagon available, and the men carried the rest on their shoulders. Many padded their shoulders with straw to cut down on chafing. Thirty hours later the rope arrived at Sackets Harbor. The men were rewarded with a barrel of whiskey and a bonus of $2 a day.

The Invasion of New York

If the results for the British at the eastern end of Lake Ontario were mixed, they fared worse in upstate New York. It was here that they launched their largest operation of the war. Sir George Prevost had received additional troops as well as some of the best generals who had served with the Duke of Wellington in Spain. Prevost was ordered to seize territory in upper New York that could be used as a bargaining chip in the peace negotiations but was also cautioned to avoid being cut off the way that Major General John Burgoyne had been in the British disaster at Saratoga in 1777.

Prevost amassed an army of 10,000 at Montreal and on August 31 crossed the border. He planned to march along the western shore of Lake Champlain as far south as Plattsburgh, which was a major American stronghold. Because Secretary of War John Armstrong did not anticipate this operation, he had ordered many of the troops here to the Niagara front. This meant that to defend Plattsburgh Brigadier General Alexander Macomb had only 3,400 men, many of whom were raw recruits.

Prevost bypassed the trees that had been cut down to slow his march and brushed aside the militia sent to contest his advance. On September 6 he arrived at Plattsburgh with about 8,000 men. Once there he sought to fix Macomb's army in place by exchanging fire with him across the Saranac River while sending a British detachment west to cross the river and threaten Macomb's rear. Prevost also waited for the outcome of a naval battle on Lake Champlain.

The Battle of Lake Champlain

Both sides had been building warships on Lake Champlain, and by the fall of 1814 the two squadrons were about evenly matched. The British squadron, commanded by thirty-six-year-old Captain George Downie, consisted of the *Confiance* (39 guns), *Linnet* (16 guns), *Chubb* (11 guns), *Finch* (11 guns) and twelve gunboats mounting a total of 17 guns. The *Confiance* was the largest ship on the lake, but she was not quite ready for action. In fact, her carpenters were still at work on her right up to the battle.

Opposing Downie was thirty-year-old Master Commandant Thomas Macdonough, whose squadron consisted of the *Saratoga* (26 guns), *Eagle* (20 guns), *Ticonderoga* (17 guns), *Preble* (7 guns), and ten gunboats carrying a total of 16 guns. Although Downie had more long guns, Macdonough had more firepower at short range with his powerful carronades. Macdonough anchored his ships in Plattsburgh

Bay and put out the kedge anchors of the *Saratoga* and *Eagle* so that he could rotate those ships around if he needed to bring fresh batteries into action. The prevailing wind favored Macdonough because the British could not easily stand off and take advantage of their long guns.

At 8:00 a.m. on September 11, Downie rounded Cumberland Head and made for Macdonough's squadron. Once within range the two squadrons pounded one another with broadsides. Both commanding officers were hit. Downie was killed fifteen minutes into the battle when he was struck by a big gun knocked from its carriage. There was not a mark on his body, but the crystal of his pocket watch was broken, marking the exact time of his death. Macdonough was twice knocked down by flying debris, once by the decapitated head of a midshipman.

The two flagships, *Confiance* and *Saratoga,* did most of the fighting, and eventually almost the entire broadside facing the enemy on each ship was out of action. At this point, Macdonough performed the masterstroke of the battle, winding *Saratoga* around so that he could bring a fresh broadside into action. Lieutenant James Robertson, who had assumed command after Downie's death, tried to do the same with the *Confiance*, but without setting his anchors in advance, his lines became fouled and his ship immobilized.

Saratoga now blasted *Confiance* with one broadside after another. A British marine who had been in the Battle of Trafalgar claimed "that was a mere flea-bite in comparison with this." Two and a half hours into the battle, *Confiance* had 105 shot-holes in her hull, and her crew went below, refusing to fight anymore. According to Lieutenant Robertson, "the ship's company declared they would stand no longer to their quarters, nor could the officers with their utmost exertions rally them." Robertson had little choice but to surrender his flagship, and the other British ships followed suit. For the second time in the war, the U.S. Navy had beaten a British squadron on an inland lake.

Although the detachment that Prevost had sent west was now on the verge of overrunning Macomb's rear, the governor-general ordered a general retreat as soon as he learned of the British defeat on Lake Champlain. Militia had been pouring into the war zone, and with the Americans now in control of the lake, Prevost feared that he might be cut off. Although his decision was probably wise, it infuriated Prevost's generals, and the governor's enemies now ganged up on him. Recalled home, he demanded a court martial to vindicate his reputation, but he died before the court convened. Macomb and Macdonough, on the other hand, were treated like heroes for defeating a British squadron and driving a major enemy force from U.S. territory.

The victory at Plattsburgh marked the end of major operations on the northern frontier in 1814. Despite growing British strength, the fighting remained inconclusive. The British controlled Prairie du Chien, Mackinac Island, and Fort Niagara, while the United States controlled both banks of the Detroit River. Neither side could claim any significant conquests, and command of the lakes was divided. After three years of fighting, the war on the Canadian-American border was a stalemate.

The British Blockade Extended

The British enjoyed more success along the Atlantic coast because they could bring their mighty fleet to bear. Their most effective use of the Royal Navy continued to

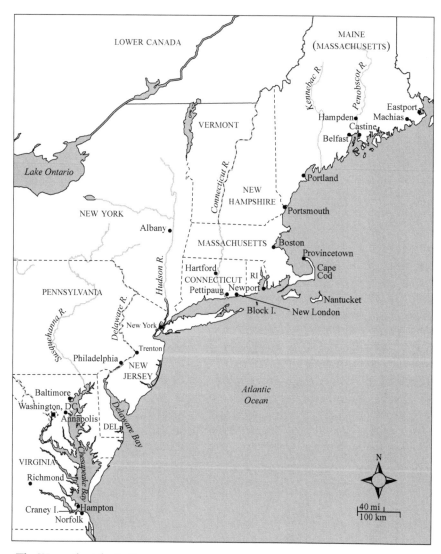

The War on the Atlantic Coast

be the blockade. The British had blockaded the ports and harbors of the middle and southern states in 1812–1813, and the blockade was extended to New England in the spring of 1814. The British targeted New England in the hope of closing ports there to U.S. warships and privateers as well as to neutral trade.

Although the British blockade now extended all the way from Maine to Georgia, it remained porous because the coast was long and irregular and the Admiralty was unwilling to devote the extensive naval resources needed to do the job right. Even so, the blockade had an enormous impact on American trade and government revenue. American exports plunged from $61 million in 1811 to $7 million in 1814 and American imports from $53 million in 1811 to $13 million in 1814. Although the taxes on trade were doubled, government revenue from all sources fell from $14 million in 1811 to $11 million in 1814. This left the Treasury far short of the funds it needed to finance the growing cost of the war.

The gluts and bottlenecks that appeared in 1813 only got worse in 1814. Merchants and fishermen could not safely send their ships to sea even if they could run the blockade, and the artisans and dockworkers who serviced the nation's commercial and fishing fleets found themselves out of work. Many farmers suffered, too, because they no longer had access to lucrative foreign markets. There were a few bright spots in the economy. Manufacturers did not have to compete with foreign producers, and a lucky privateer could still turn a profit. So, too, could farmers and domestic traders who lived near enough to a war zone to take advantage of government contracts or who were willing to deal with the enemy. For most people, however, the war brought hard times.

New England Raided

With New England now under blockade, the Royal Navy stepped up its raids along the coast. The targets were mainly small ports and fishing villages that could offer little resistance. One naval force sailed up the Connecticut River and destroyed ships worth $140,000 at Pettipaug (now Essex), Connecticut. Another bombarded Stonington, Connecticut. Exposed communities on Cape Cod came to terms with the British, paying tribute to avoid bombardment and looting.

The British presence made it impossible for coastal islands to carry on their traditional trade with the mainland. Nantucket was controlled by Republicans who supported the war, but by August 1814 the threat of starvation was so acute that the island declared its neutrality. In exchange for surrendering its public stores and ending federal tax payments, the island was permitted to trade with the mainland and fish in nearby waters. As an additional reward to the island, British naval officials promised to work for the release of Nantucketeers who were being held as prisoners of war, although the conflict ended before they could make good on this promise.

Block Island, which was part of Rhode Island, openly collaborated with the Royal Navy. According to a U.S. Navy officer, it was "in the daily habit of carrying intelligence and succor to the enemy's squadron." American officials responded by cutting off all trade with the island.

The Seizure of Maine

The British did not confine themselves to petty raids but also conducted a major amphibious operation against Maine. British officials had long coveted northern Maine because it jutted into Canada, blocking the establishment of a road that would link Quebec to Halifax. Since the peace treaty signed at the end of the American Revolution had not clearly defined the international boundary between Maine and Canada, British officials hoped that occupying the territory would lead to a favorable settlement.

On July 11 the British seized Moose Island, which was claimed by both nations but occupied by the United States. Since Royal officials regarded this as British territory, residents were forced to take an oath of allegiance or leave. Most took the oath.

In early September, Sir John Sherbrooke, the lieutenant governor of Nova Scotia, led a more ambitious campaign against coastal Maine, occupying a hundred miles of the coast from Eastport to Castine. The British confiscated all public property in the occupied territory and forced the residents to take an oath to keep the peace or leave. Those willing to take an additional oath of allegiance to the Crown were permitted to trade with British ports. Most residents welcomed the British occupation because it meant unfettered trade with New Brunswick and Nova Scotia. Castine became a British port of entry and a popular destination for British officers on leave, and money flowed into Maine.

American officials cut off mail service to the occupied territory and hatched a plan for re-conquest. Maine was then part of Massachusetts, and the plan called for attacking overland, relying heavily on militia and money supplied by the Bay State. But Massachusetts was in the throes of a war-induced depression and thus was strapped for funds. In addition, Governor Caleb Strong's advisors told him (probably correctly) that the operation was unlikely to succeed without naval control of the Bay of Penobscot. The administration had to scrap the plan anyway when it was leaked to the press. As a result, coastal Maine remained in British hands until the war ended.

More British Raids in the Chesapeake

Far more devastating than the occupation of Maine was the British resumption of raids in the Chesapeake. The British had enjoyed considerable success in the Chesapeake in 1813, and the renewal of raids there was designed to bring the war home to Americans and to retaliate for U.S. depredations in Upper Canada. The British also hoped to draw off American troops from northern frontier, but the administration preferred to rely on local forces to defend against the British raids.

After establishing a base on Tangier Island in April, the British in June launched a series of petty raids, targeting mostly small villages and plantations on Maryland's western shore, burning houses and barns and carrying off property. As in 1813, the British met with little resistance. Few regulars were available, and local militia units either showed up late, were pounded by British warships, or were swept aside by British landing parties.

The Navy Department sought to counter the raids with a flotilla of barges and gunboats under the command of Captain Joshua Barney, a Revolutionary War hero and successful privateering commander. Although Barney's flotilla engaged in several battles with British ships, eventually it was bottled up above Pig Point on the Patuxent River and had to be blown up to keep it out of British hands.

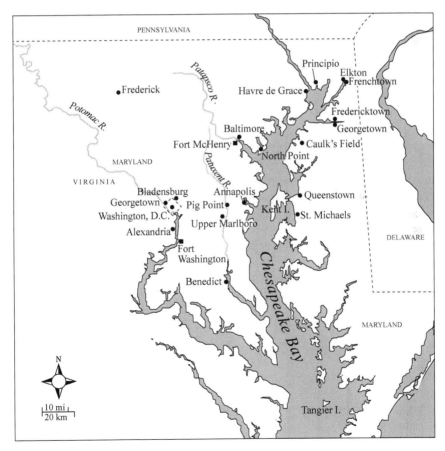

The War in the Chesapeake

The property losses from the British raids were heavy. No less troubling was the prospect of a British-induced slave revolt. Ever since 1813 runaway slaves had sought sanctuary on British warships or in British camps, and British officials refused to forcefully return those who wished to remain. Then on April 2, 1814, Vice Admiral Alexander Cochrane issued a proclamation openly inviting slaves to join the British cause. Cochrane offered all interested Americans a "choice of either entering into His Majesty's sea or land forces or being sent as FREE settlers to the British possessions in North America or the West Indies." In the course of the war, some 3,600 slaves responded to the British call.

Around 550 of the runaways joined a special Corps of Colonial Marines. The new recruits made excellent scouts and guides because they knew the terrain. They also proved themselves in combat. Since capture meant sure death, there was no temptation to surrender. Rear Admiral George Cockburn claimed that they made "the best skirmishers possible for the thick woods of the country" and that they showed "extraordinary steadiness and good conduct when in action with the enemy."

Washington Targeted

Some of the British raids were conducted perilously close to the nation's capital, but little was done to provide for its defense. Secretary of War John Armstrong thought the British would target Baltimore instead, and other officials in the administration were slow to see the danger. Not until July 1 did President Madison create a special military district embracing Washington and put Brigadier General William Winder in charge. Winder had fought on the Niagara frontier but without distinction. After being captured at Stoney Creek, he was exchanged and had returned to Maryland, where his brother served as governor. Winder seemed overwhelmed by the task before him and spent most of his time galloping through the countryside to inspect terrain, while the real work of establishing defenses around Washington remained undone.

In August Vice Admiral Cochrane arrived with several transports full of veterans from the Spanish Peninsula under the command of Major General Robert Ross. Also present was Rear Admiral Cockburn, who had shown a talent for amphibious warfare in the Chesapeake the previous year and was eager to target the U.S. capital. After sailing up the Patuxent, Ross landed with 4,500 troops at Benedict and then marched to Upper Marlboro, where he was joined by Cockburn. By this time, Cochrane, who remained with the fleet, had gotten cold feet and urged a withdrawal, but with Cockburn's encouragement, Ross marched on to Bladensburg, where he could cross the Eastern Branch of the Potomac (now the Anacostia River) and approach Washington from the northeast.

Finally aware of the danger, American officials frantically sought to prepare to meet the British advance. Winder had about 6,000 men at his disposal. Although mostly militia, his force included 500 regulars and, more importantly, 600 seamen and marines who had arrived from Pig Point with Barney after their flotilla was blown up. Barney rounded up five pieces of heavy artillery (three 12-pounders and two 18-pounders), which provided the heart of American firepower at Bladensburg.

Winder arrayed his troops in three lines on the Washington side of the Eastern Branch of the Potomac. The third line was too far away to support the first two lines, and Secretary of State James Monroe (who had no authority in the matter) redeployed the second line so that it could not support the first. President Madison arrived with an entourage and was on the verge of crossing the river when the British columns appeared in sight. The 100-degree temperatures caused problems on both sides, the British losing some men on their march to heat exhaustion.

The British reached the river about 1:00 p.m. on August 24. Although the bridge across the river had not been destroyed, the water was shallow enough to ford. Despite taking heavy casualties, the British poured across the bridge, and after outflanking the first American line forced it to fall back. Winder, who radiated confusion and defeatism from the outset, ordered the second line to fall back, and what was supposed to be an orderly withdrawal to a new position turned into a rout, immortalized in song and poetry as "the Bladensburg races." The British use of Congreve rockets probably contributed to the panic.

Only Barney's seamen and marines, who anchored the third line, held firm, tearing large gaps in the advancing British columns with their heavy guns. But the British drove off the militia protecting Barney's flank and stormed his position. By now Barney was out of ammunition and ordered his men to flee, but since he was wounded he remained in place and was captured. Out of respect for his fighting ability, both afloat and ashore, the British high command showed him every courtesy and released him on parole. The Battle of Bladensburg had lasted about three hours, with the British sustaining some 250 casualties to only 70 for the United States. As these figures suggest, the Republic might have prevailed with a more dependable force.

By the time the Battle of Bladensburg was under way, Washington had begun to empty out, and when news of the rout reached the Capital, most of the remaining residents fled. Wagons and carriages were at a premium, and Dolley Madison sacrificed her personal property to save White House treasures, including a portrait of George Washington painted by Gilbert Stuart. The president returned to the White House after his wife had left. Although the secretary of the treasury had given him two matched pistols, Madison left them in the White House, and they disappeared, stolen, probably, by local predators who slipped in after the president had left.

Ross rested his exhausted troops for a couple of hours before marching them into Washington. He and Cockburn looked in vain for someone to surrender the city. The British took sniper fire from a house, which they torched, but otherwise there was no resistance. Cockburn led a group of officers into the White House. After consuming some food and wine that had been laid out for an afternoon meal, they took some souvenirs and then burned the building. All that survived was a shell. They also torched the Capitol Building and the building housing the State and Treasury departments as well as the arsenal on Greenleaf's Point. Captain Thomas Tingey, who was superintendent of the Washington Navy Yard, the best-stocked yard in the nation, burned it as well as two fine ships on the stocks when the British entered the city.

The British were remarkably respectful of civilians who remained in the city, and they left most private property alone, although they made several exceptions. They burned a couple of ropewalks that were under contract to the government, and Cockburn threatened to torch the office of the semi-official Washington *National Intelligencer.* He settled for destroying its contents after neighbors convinced him that a fire would endanger their homes. Dr. William Thornton, the superintendent of patents, saved the patent office by persuading the British that the models inside were private property and that to destroy them would render the British as infamous as the Turks who burned the library at Alexandria in antiquity. The U.S. Marine Corps buildings were also spared but only because the British did not realize what they were.

The fires in Washington burned all night and could be seen from miles around. They were doused by a pair of ferocious storms that hit the city that night, one of them blowing down a building and killing British soldiers inside. Other British soldiers, perhaps as many as seventy-five, were killed or wounded when a dry well filled with 130 barrels of powder exploded, leaving a hole that was forty feet wide. The British departed from the city the next day. Barney agreed to look after the wounded they left behind.

The British were criticized on both sides of the Atlantic for the burning of Washington. "The Cossacks spared Paris," commented the London *Statesman,* alluding to the Russian occupation at the end of Napoleon's reign, "but we spared not the capital of America." Most British subjects, however, welcomed the news. The Prince Regent called the Chesapeake campaign "brilliant and successful," and newspapers in London were reportedly unhappy "that [British] commanders did not date their dispatches from the Capitol."

In the United States, there was some grumbling against the president. Graffiti appeared on the Capitol's charred walls that read: "George Washington founded this city after a seven years' war with England—James Madison lost it after a two years' war." Secretary of War John Armstrong, however, took most of the heat. He had alienated everyone in the cabinet, and Monroe, who saw him as a competitor for the presidency, was a particularly unrelenting foe. Militia refused to take orders from Armstrong, and many locals believed that as a northerner he had purposely sacrificed the city. He was forced to resign. Monroe eventually replaced him, although the Virginian continued to serve as secretary of state on an interim basis.

The Surrender of Alexandria

The United States suffered another humiliating setback shortly after the fall of Washington. This was the surrender of Alexandria. Captain James Gordon had led a squadron up the Potomac to support the operation against Washington. Forced to contend with shallows and contrary winds, Gordon did not reach Fort Washington until two days after the British had abandoned the capital, but instead of offering resistance, the commander of the fort blew it up and fled. This left Alexandria, an affluent Federalist city upriver, exposed.

Alexandria formally surrendered, turning over all its public stores and maritime wealth to the British. Gordon left with twenty-seven prize ships filled with booty. His return downriver was harrowing. He had to contend with more shallows and with American fire ships as well as artillery and small arms fire, but he made it safely to the mouth of the river with his prize goods intact. One British naval officer called Gordon's operation "as brilliant an achievement . . . as grace the annals of our naval history."

The Battle for Baltimore

The occupation of the capital was undoubtedly the low point for the United States in the war, but it was soon followed by a high point: the successful defense of Baltimore. The British targeted the city because it was wealthy, fiercely anti-British, and the home port for many privateers. However, ever since 1813 Samuel Smith, a U.S. senator and a major general in the militia, had been beefing up its defenses. By the time the British threatened it, the Monument City had established extensive earthworks to the east that were manned by some 10,000 to 15,000 militia.

Before attacking the city Vice Admiral Cochrane sent a naval force to the Eastern Shore to keep the militia busy there. Heading the expedition was a popular twenty-nine-year-old naval captain, Sir Peter Parker, who belonged to a prominent naval family and was the poet Lord Byron's cousin. On August 31 Parker landed and marched to a militia camp near Georgetown that was under the command of Lieutenant Colonel Philip Reed, a U.S. senator and Revolutionary War veteran. In the ensuing engagement, the militia made a good showing, taking a heavy toll on Parker's advancing force.

The battle ended when Parker went down with what proved to be a fatal leg wound. With this the British withdrew to their ship. Reed's militia had sustained only three casualties compared to forty for the British. Not only had Reed's citizen soldiers bested a veteran British force, but the Royal Navy was deprived of one of its rising stars, who was subsequently eulogized by Byron. The Battle of Caulk's Field was of no strategic value, but when word of it spread, it gave a boost to American morale.

For the assault on Baltimore, Major General Ross landed the main British force, 4,500 men, on September 12 at North Point, about fourteen miles from the city. Halfway to the city the British ran into 3,200 militia under Brigadier General John Stricker. When Ross raced ahead to investigate, he was killed by enemy fire. Colonel Arthur Brooke took command and forced the militia to withdraw. However, in the Battle of North Point the British suffered 340 casualties to only 215 for the United States. They had also lost one of their most popular and gifted officers. As a general officer, Ross was entitled to be buried at home, and his remains were shipped there in a barrel of rum.

Brooke proceeded to the outskirts of Baltimore but found the defenses too formidable to attack without naval support. Cochrane personally led a squadron of bomb and rocket ships up the Patapsco River to Fort McHenry, which he had to subdue in order to get close enough to reach the American lines with his big naval guns. Over a twenty-five hour period Cochrane's squadron fired some 1,500 rounds at the fort, but only 400 found their mark, and only four Americans were killed and another twenty-four wounded. Unable to force the fort to submit, Cochrane gave up the assault. By this time Brooke had already pulled back his troops. Baltimore was thus saved.

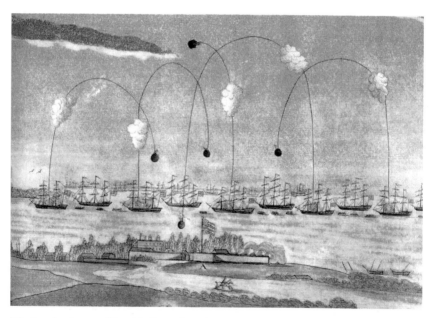

The bombardment of Fort McHenry in 1814 produced "The Star-Spangled Banner." (Drawing by John Bower. Library of Congress)

The Flag and the Song

The bombardment of Fort McHenry was witnessed by Francis Scott Key, who was on board a truce ship under the guns of the main British fleet eight or nine miles away at the mouth of the Patapsco. Key had gone to the British fleet to secure the release of Dr. William Beanes, a civilian the British had seized. By the time that Key arrived, the British had already decided to release Beanes, but the Americans were not permitted to leave until the assault on Fort McHenry was over.

Key paced all night watching the bombardment of the fort from afar. When he saw the British squadron returning downriver on the morning of September 14, he knew the fort had survived. This was confirmed shortly thereafter when he saw (probably through a spyglass) the fort's huge flag (which was thirty by forty-two feet) run up to the tune of "Yankee Doodle." Key was so moved that he wrote a song that could be sung to the tune of a British drinking song, "To Anacreon in Heaven." Initially entitled "The Defence of Fort McHenry," it was later re-titled "The Star-Spangled Banner." ("The bombs bursting in air" were British mortar shells that exploded over the fort, and "the rockets' red glare" were Congreve rockets fired at the fort.) Key's tune became a hit, and in 1931 Congress proclaimed it the national anthem.

As for the huge Fort McHenry flag, it remained in the family of Major George Armistead, the commander of the fort during the bombardment, for the rest of the century. The family periodically cut off patches to give away as souvenirs but donated the flag to the Smithsonian Institution in the twentieth century. Thus, a campaign in the Chesapeake that had been marked by the burning of the public buildings in Washington and the ignominious surrender of Alexandria ended with the successful defense of Baltimore, and in the process produced two powerful symbols, a song and a flag, that resonated through the nation's history.

Cumberland Island

Although the British launched their principal amphibious operations against New England and the Chesapeake, Cumberland Island at the mouth of St. Marys River in Georgia was also targeted. This operation was launched in early 1815 as a diversion to Great Britain's Gulf Coast campaign against New Orleans. The two sites were separated by nearly 600 miles of wilderness, which suggests that the British did not fully appreciate the immense scope of the new nation.

The operation began on January 10–11, when Rear Admiral Cockburn landed some 1,500 men on the island. On January 13 the British attacked 120 U.S. regulars commanded by Captain Abraham Massias who were defending Point Peter. The Americans resisted as long as they could and then fled upriver. When Cockburn sent a detachment upriver the following month, it had to turn back when it was ambushed from both sides at a point where the river narrows. Casualties in the two engagements in the Cumberland Island operation were light. The British occupation of Cumberland Island had no impact on the Gulf Coast campaign and actually took place after the Battle of New Orleans was fought, but the British retained control of the island until the war ended several weeks later.

Britain's Gulf Coast Campaign

The last British campaign of the war targeted the Gulf Coast. As early as 1812 Sir George Prevost had suggested such a campaign to take the pressure off of Canada, although by the time it got under way in 1814 the British were mainly interested in occupying territory that would improve their bargaining position in the peace negotiations. The British planned to take advantage of potential dissidents in the region—Indians, blacks (slave and free), and any of the French or Spanish unhappy with American rule—but they showed no interest in making Louisiana independent or in restoring it to Spain.

Britain's principal target on the Gulf Coast was New Orleans. Located one hundred miles up the Mississippi River, the city boasted 25,000 people. It was not only the largest city west of the Appalachians but also the principal outlet for western produce, which was floated down the Mississippi River in barges and then transferred to oceangoing vessels at New Orleans. By 1814 the warehouses in New Orleans were filled with commodities because the war had made oceangoing voyages too dangerous. Control of New Orleans offered the British not only a commanding position on the most important river in the West but also the prospect of considerable prize money.

Although the British sent arms to Indians on the Gulf Coast in May 1814, by then the Creek War was over, and the Indians who remained hostile to the United States were unpromising allies. The next step was to establish a position at Pensacola, a Spanish port city that offered the best harbor in the region and excellent access to the interior. With the tacit approval of Spanish officials in the city, the British in August occupied the forts in the bay. The following month the British targeted Mobile, a port city in West Florida that the United States had taken from Spain in 1813. The city was protected by Fort Bowyer, which was garrisoned by 160 regulars commanded by Major William Lawrence. But the British land force was not big enough to take the fort, and when the British flagship ran aground within range of the fort's guns and had to be destroyed, the attack was abandoned.

Andrew Jackson, who was now a major general in the U.S. Army, had assumed command of the region in May 1814. Convinced that Pensacola was the key to British operations, he was determined to neutralize the city. Although Washington officials had ordered Jackson not to invade Spanish territory, the directive arrived too late to affect his plans. On November 7, Jackson marched some 4,000 troops into Pensacola. Spanish officials, unsure of what to do, offered no resistance. Disgusted with this turn of events, the British blew up the city's forts and retired to a base they had established on the Apalachicola River more than 150 miles to the east. With the forts destroyed, Pensacola was neutralized, and Jackson marched to Mobile and then New Orleans, arriving at the Crescent City on December 1.

Defense of New Orleans

New Orleans was wholly unprepared to defend itself. Most of the people living there were of French or Spanish descent, and preferring their old European masters, saw no reason to put their lives on the line for the United States. There was also a scarcity of cash in the city, and the banks were unwilling to lend what little they had to the government. "*Few, very few,*" lamented a U.S. Army officer, "are disposed to aid the General Government in the present crisis."

Jackson's arrival, however, had a dramatic effect. "General Jackson," wrote one contemporary, "electrified all hearts." After making a detailed study of the area, Jackson blocked the approaches to New Orleans, established an intelligence system, and issued a proclamation calling upon everyone to aid in the defense of the city. "Those who are not for us," he said, "are against us and will be dealt with accordingly."

Governor William Claiborne called out militia from the surrounding area, and Brigadier General John Coffee raced 850 mounted Tennessee riflemen in from Baton Rouge, covering 135 miles in three days. Jackson had begun enlisting free blacks into the army, and now, over white objections, he accepted the services of a special corps of free blacks, mostly refugees from Santo Domingo, raised by Captain Jean Baptiste Savary.

The Baratarian pirates, headed by Jean and Pierre Laffite, also offered their services. Although the navy had destroyed their base on Grand Terre Island in September, the Baratarians rejected British overtures and sought to escape criminal charges by throwing their lot in with the United States. Jackson had earlier called them "hellish banditti," but he needed the Baratarians' manpower, artillery expertise, and knowledge of the surrounding area, and so he accepted their offer. Jackson got on well with Jean Laffite, who became his unofficial aide-de-camp.

The Battle of Lake Borgne

Meanwhile, the British had been assembling a large army, about 10,000 strong, in Jamaica for the campaign. The command was assigned to Major General Edward Pakenham, an accomplished officer who was Wellington's brother-in-law. At the end of November, the troops boarded transports in a large convoy—commanded by Cochrane—and sailed to the Gulf Coast.

Because they lacked enough small boats to attack further north, the British decided to approach New Orleans via Lake Borgne. Blocking their way at the eastern end of the lake was a flotilla of five U.S. gunboats manned by 185 men under the command of Lieutenant Thomas ap Catesby Jones. Although Jones was supposed to keep an eye out for the British rather than engage them, he lost his wind and had little choice but to prepare for battle. The British approached on December 14 in forty-five small boats manned by 1,200 men and commanded by Captain Nicholas Lockyer. In the Battle of Lake Borgne, British manpower and firepower carried the day. Jones was wounded and his flotilla was defeated and captured.

Three Preliminary Engagements

After establishing a base on Pea Island, the British followed a series of bayous and canals to Jaques Villieré's plantation, which was located on the Mississippi River about eight miles south of New Orleans. On December 23, some 1,600 British soldiers led by Colonel William Thornton occupied the plantation. Although they captured thirty militia at the plantation, Villieré's son escaped to warn Jackson of the British approach.

Jackson wasted no time in challenging the British. Determined to meet them beyond New Orleans and before they were at full strength, he led 1,800 men to within a mile of the plantation. He was supported by two warships, the *Carolina* (14 guns) and a converted merchantman, the *Louisiana* (22 guns). At 7:30 in the evening of December 23, the *Carolina* opened fire on the British camp, and shortly thereafter Jackson attacked. The British, who were now under the command of Major General Thomas Keane, were caught by surprise. In the Battle of Villieré's Plantation, there were numerous bayonet wounds from the close combat. The lines were not clearly drawn, and in the darkness, smoke, and fog, there were some casualties from friendly fire. Before pulling back, Jackson had inflicted 275 casualties on the British while sustaining 215.

Pakenham arrived two days later (on Christmas Day) with reinforcements. To neutralize the American ships, which continued to harass his troops, the British commander ordered a furnace for hot shot built and on December 27 launched an artillery barrage that destroyed the *Carolina* when it caught fire and blew up. Meanwhile, Jackson built a line of earthworks behind a canal that stretched from the river to a cypress swamp in the east. At the same time, Tennessee and Choctaw sharpshooters sniped at British pickets, a form of warfare that the British considered "an ungenerous return to barbarity."

On December 28, Pakenham ordered an advance in force but suffered such intense fire from the American line as well as from the *Louisiana* (which fired 800 rounds) that he ordered a retreat. In this engagement, known as the British Reconnaissance in Force, the casualties were light, perhaps thirty-five for the Americans and fifty-five for the British. Jackson used the lull that followed to good advantage, extending his line deeper into the swamp and establishing additional artillery batteries in the line, bringing the total to eight.

On January 1, 1815, there was yet another engagement, an artillery exchange known as the Battle of Rodrigues Canal (or the Artillery Duel). The British, however, were at a disadvantage because Jackson's batteries were behind such strong earthworks and the Americans had far more ammunition at their disposal. After two and a half hours, the British had lost a battery to American fire and run out of ammunition. Hence, they pulled back. The British had suffered seventy-five casualties, the Americans thirty-five.

The Battle of New Orleans

These preliminary engagements were followed by the main battle on January 8. The British plan called for Colonel Thornton to lead a brigade across the river, overrun several batteries that Jackson had established there, and turn the guns on Jackson's main line. At the same time, Pakenham would direct a frontal assault with about 5,300 men against Jackson's line, which was defended by 4,700 men.

The British plan went awry from the beginning. Thornton fell behind schedule, and although his men routed the Americans on the east bank and gained control of the guns, by then the main British attack on the west bank had stalled and Thornton was ordered to withdraw.

Pakenham's advance on the west bank was initially covered by fog, but the air soon cleared, and Jackson's artillery opened fire, tearing large holes in the advancing British lines. When the British got closer they suffered galling fire from Jackson's riflemen and musketeers. An American participant said that "the atmosphere was filled with sheets of fire and volumes of smoke," and a British veteran of the Napoleonic Wars called the fire "the most murderous I ever beheld before or since."

The Americans enjoyed good cover behind their earthworks, while the British were cut down before they could get near. Only a small column of men advancing along the riverbank reached the American line, but heavy fire forced these troops to fall back. Pakenham made a conspicuous target as he rode across the field encouraging his men, and he was "cut asunder by a cannon ball." Major General John Lambert took command and broke off the engagement, which had lasted only a half hour. Some British soldiers who had thrown themselves on the ground in the heat of the battle now got up and surrendered. Americans who viewed the battlefield were appalled by what they saw, the "dead and wounded laying in heaps"—all dressed in scarlet British uniforms.

The Battle of New Orleans was the last major battle of the war. It was also the largest and bloodiest battle and produced the most lopsided outcome. The British

This illustration of the Battle of New Orleans shows how exposed the advancing British troops were, particularly to the deadly fire of the artillery batteries that anchored Jackson's line. (Drawing by A. Hotzy. Lithograph by P. S. Duval. *United States Military Magazine,* 1841)

lost over 2,000 men (including 500 captured), while Jackson sustained only seventy casualties and only thirteen on the east side of the river.

Jackson's Dictatorship

Although the British remained active on the Gulf Coast, bombarding Fort St. Philip downstream from New Orleans and seizing Fort Bowyer in Mobile Bay, they were unlikely to attack New Orleans again. Nevertheless, Jackson was reluctant to loosen his grip on the Crescent City. He had proclaimed martial law on December 16 to prevent spies from moving freely in and out of the city, and although reports filtered into New Orleans of the restoration of peace as early as February 19, Jackson refused to lift martial law until official news arrived on March 13. In the meantime, a member of the state legislature wrote a newspaper article complaining, and Jackson ordered him jailed. When a federal judge ordered the victim released Jackson jailed the judge. After the war ended, the judge hauled Jackson into court, where he was convicted of contempt and fined $1,000. (In 1844 Congress refunded the fine with interest—$2,733 in all—after the aging hero of New Orleans had come upon hard times.)

Jackson also dealt severely with 200 Tennessee militiamen who had gone home in September 1814 because they thought their tour of duty was up. Jackson ordered the men arrested and tried by a military court, which found them guilty. Most forfeited some pay, had to make up for time lost, and then were drummed out of camp with their heads partly shaved. Six ringleaders, however, who were convicted of mutiny as well as desertion, were sentenced to death. They were executed by firing squad on February 21, 1815, Jackson refusing to show any mercy despite the fact that the war appeared to be over. The Battle of New Orleans made Jackson a national hero, but his enemies never let the public forget his severe brand of military justice.

Last Naval Engagements

There were fewer naval engagements on the high seas in 1814 because most U.S. warships were bottled up in port by the British blockade. Even so, the United States suffered losses both inland and at sea. The British occupation of Washington forced the destruction of two ships that were on the stocks at the navy yard, and the British conquest of eastern Maine led to the destruction of the U.S. sloop *Adams* to prevent it from falling into enemy hands. The United States also lost two frigates to British warships on the high seas.

Captain David Porter had sailed the U.S. frigate *Essex* (46 guns) into the Pacific in late 1812. Thereafter, he cruised against British whaling ships and lived off the enemy. In 1813 the British sent a small squadron after Porter. Two of the British ships, the *Phoebe* (mounting 46 or 53 guns) and the *Cherub* (26 guns), caught up with the *Essex* at Valparaiso, Chile. On March 28, 1814, Porter made a run for open waters, but a sudden squall destroyed his topmast. Although he took refuge in Chilean waters, the two British ships attacked. Porter resisted as long as he could but then had to surrender. The American captain bitterly assailed the British for attacking him in neutral waters, while the British criticized Porter for conniving in the escape of his crew after he had surrendered.

The United States also lost one of its heavy frigates, the *President* (53 guns). Commanded by Captain Stephen Decatur, this ship slipped out of New York Harbor during a snow storm on January 14, 1815. Although considered a good sailer, the *President* ran aground and got so twisted around before breaking free that she evidently lost some of her sailing qualities. The *President* was subsequently chased by a squadron of British ships that included the heavy frigate *Endymion* (47 guns) and two light frigates. The *Endymion* was known for her speed, and her captain, Henry Hope, made the most of it. He got on Decatur's starboard quarter and repeatedly pounded the American ship, inflicting considerable damage. Although Decatur eventually knocked the *Endymion* out of action, he had sustained so much damage that he surrendered to the two trailing British frigates.

The *Constitution* (52 guns), on the other hand, continued her run of good luck. Commanded by Captain Charles Stewart, she escaped from Boston Harbor in December 1814. On February 20, 1815, she ran into two British ships, the *Cyane* (33 guns) and the *Levant* (21 guns), 200 miles from Madeira. Although the British ships were outclassed, their commanders were so confident of their seamanship that they engaged the *Constitution*. Stewart handled his ship extremely well, and his men showed superb gunnery. The American ship raked both British ships, compelling them to surrender. Although subsequently chased by a British squadron, "Old Ironsides" made it safely back to port with its reputation much enhanced.

The United States constructed six new sloops during the war. In 1814, three—the *Hornet* (20 guns), *Peacock* (22 guns), and *Wasp* (22 guns)—enjoyed successful cruises. Between them they defeated several British warships, including the *Penguin* and *Reindeer* (each carrying 19 guns), the *Avon* (20 guns), and the *Epervier* (18 guns). The British, in turn, captured the *Frolic* (22 guns), *Syren* (16 guns), and *Rattlesnake* (16 guns). The *Wasp* was lost at sea, probably in a storm, taking all hands with her.

In October 1814, Robert Fulton launched the first steam frigate, which he called *Demologos* but was later named *Fulton the First*. Although designed to protect New York Harbor, she was not ready for service until after the war was over. Fulton and others also experimented with submarines and mines (which contemporaries called "torpedoes"). Several attempts were made to use crude submarines to attach mines to British warships but without success. The United States also launched two ships-of-the-line in 1814, the *Independence* in June and the *Washington* in October, but both were poorly designed and neither was ready for sea before the war ended.

The War on British Commerce

American warships and privateers continued their war on British commerce in 1814–1815. According to the British *Naval Chronicle*, "The depredations committed on our commerce by American ships of war and privateers has attained an extent beyond all former precedent." Insurance rates for British ships trading between Liverpool and Halifax soared to 30 percent of the value of the ship and cargo, and underwriters publicly complained about their losses. "Each daily book [of losses] at Lloyds [the principal insurer]," said one, "presents a *tremendous* list for our contemplation."

The favorite haunt of American privateers in 1814 was the British Isles because ships in those waters were not required to sail in convoy. Privateers took prizes and "in summer weather and light breezes eluded all attempts of the king's ships to catch them." American privateers made commerce in the Irish Sea so dangerous that insurance rates for ships trading between England and Ireland soared to 13 percent. According to the *Naval Chronicle,* this was *"three times higher"* than it was when we were at war with all Europe!"

Several American privateers enjoyed especially successful cruises in 1814. The *Prince-de-Neufchatel* (mounting 17 guns) captured or destroyed $1 million in British property in a single cruise. The *Governor Tompkins* (14 guns) stripped and burned fourteen prizes in the English Channel, while the *Harpy* (14 guns) returned to the United States after a twenty-day cruise with booty worth more than $400,000. Captain Thomas Boyle, who commanded the *Chasseur* (16 guns)—"the pride of Baltimore"—added insult to injury by sailing into a British port and issuing a proclamation that mocked British blockade notices. Boyle proclaimed a blockade of "all the ports, harbors, bays, creeks, rivers, inlets, outlets, islands, and sea coast of the United Kingdom of G. Britain and Ireland."

Normally, privateers fled from British warships and when cornered surrendered, but there were some exceptions. In September 1814, boats from a British squadron repeatedly attacked the *General Armstrong* (14 guns) when she was anchored in the Azores. Although the privateer ultimately had to be abandoned, the British sustained so many casualties (200 to only nine for the Americans) that Royal Navy officers would not permit mail on the vessels that carried their wounded home.

The following month the *Endymion* (47 guns) was becalmed near Nantucket within sight of the *Prince-de-Neufchatel* (17 guns). The American privateer had manned so many prizes that her crew was down to forty men. Nevertheless, she beat off an attack from the boats of the *Endymion,* inflicting one hundred casualties while sustaining only thirty. Although the *Prince* was left with only ten healthy seamen, she managed to slip away and reach home safely.

Equally impressive was a duel that the *Chasseur,* now carrying 14 guns but still commanded by Boyle, engaged in. On February 26, 1815, the Chasseur encountered the British schooner *St. Lawrence* (15 guns). Mistaking the British warship for an armed merchantman, Boyle attacked. After a fifteen-minute engagement, the *St. Lawrence* struck its colors. This was an unusual case, for the Royal Navy captured a great many American privateers. But those that remained free to cruise continued to harass British trade until the war was over.

Results of the Campaign

All in all, the United States had done pretty well in the campaign of 1814. Although the British retained Mackinac and Prairie du Chien, the United States remained in the ascendant in the Old Northwest, and it had made a good showing on the Niagara even though little of strategic consequence was achieved. Further east, the Republic was thrown on the defensive but compelled the British to withdraw from New York and abandon its assault on Baltimore. The only significant British successes were the conquest of eastern Maine and the capture and burning of Washington, and as demoralizing and humiliating as the latter was, it was largely offset by Jackson's spectacular victory at New Orleans.

American success in 1814–1815 was partly the result of improved leadership and better troops in the field. Brown and Scott on the Niagara, Macomb and Macdonough at Plattsburgh, and Jackson at New Orleans had all demonstrated a talent for command and a taste for combat. After two years of campaigning, Madison had finally found the right men to fight his war.

In all three campaigns (1812, 1813, and 1814), the defending side had fared better than the attacking side. This was largely a function of the logistical environment. Offensive operations required moving men and material over rough terrain with few good roads or serviceable waterways. Defending armies, by contrast, could dig in and take advantage of shorter supply lines. Thus, after three years of campaigning, neither side could claim victory. On the battlefield, the War of 1812 ended in a draw.

Chapter 5

The Inner War

The War of 1812 had seven major theaters of operation in North America: (1) the Detroit frontier, (2) the Niagara frontier, (3) the St. Lawrence front, (4) the Lake Champlain-Richelieu River front, (5) the Chesapeake, (6) the Southwest (seat of the Creek War), and (7) the Gulf Coast. There was an eighth front on the high seas. For Americans, another front also loomed large. This was the home front, where people debated the merits of the war, argued over policy and strategy, and maneuvered for preference or advantage.

The nation's internal differences went far beyond the norm and had an impact on the prosecution of the war. There was bickering, backbiting, and disloyalty in the cabinet; the administration quarreled with Congress; Republicans in Congress feuded with each other; and Republicans everywhere fought with Federalists. This "inner war" cast a cloud over the entire war effort. What happened in Washington and the state capitals influenced the course of the war as much as what happened in the field.

Policy and Politics

The inner war was in part a product of legitimate differences of opinion. Was the war just and winnable, or was it an ill-advised invitation to disaster? Should Canada be targeted because the British were vulnerable there, or should the war be confined to the high seas because that is where the encroachments on American rights occurred? Should the nation raise long-term regulars, or should it rely on short-term volunteers and militia? Should it build ships-of-the-line and frigates that could challenge the Royal Navy, or should it build sloops that could target British commerce? Or should the nation leave the war on the high seas to privateers and devote its limited naval resources to taking control of the inland lakes in order to support land operations? Should the war be financed with taxes, or should the nation rely instead on loans and paper money? Were trade restrictions an aid in prosecuting the war, or were they a hindrance? These were questions over which honest men could differ.

Politics also played a part in the inner war. Hoping to lay claim to the victories and avoid blame for the defeats, individuals maneuvered accordingly. Republicans hoped for victories that would vindicate their war policy and assure their continued success at the polls, while Federalists were convinced that failure would open the public's eyes and restore them to power. Despite the nation's peril, political considerations were never far from the surface and could never be entirely divorced from the policy decisions that had to be made.

The disputes within the president's cabinet were sometimes grounded on policy, but often they were personal and political. Monroe was jealous of Armstrong because he saw him as a potential rival for the presidency, and Armstrong alienated everyone with his arrogance. Postmaster General Gideon Granger was sympathetic to dissident Republicans and filled positions at his disposal with men who were openly hostile to the administration. A stronger president might have demanded more loyalty and imposed more unity, but that was not Madison's style. As a result, he was not quite master of his own house.

Republicans in Congress were also deeply divided. The War Hawks and regular Republicans often differed on policy matters, and other factions—the Old Republicans, Clintonians, and Senate "Invisibles"—openly defied the administration and torpedoed its policies. The regular Republicans sometimes found the independence of the dissidents more exasperating than the opposition of the Federalists. As one administration supporter put it, "The malcontent junto of self-styled Republicans was worse" than the Federalists.

Election of 1812

Factionalism played a significant role in the election of 1812 and very nearly cost Madison the presidency. Although voters usually rally around a wartime president, Madison fared worse in 1812 than he had in 1808. Many people, Federalists and Republicans alike, wondered if "Little Jemmy" (who was only five feet four inches tall) was big enough for the job.

The presidential campaign opened in February 1812 when Republicans in the Virginia legislature nominated electors committed to Madison. In the ensuing months Republican caucuses in seven other states followed suit. In May the Republican caucus in Congress added its endorsement, although Republican congressmen from New York and other northern states withheld their support. When the New York legislature endorsed De Witt Clinton, the talented and popular mayor of New York City, he became the opposition candidate. He won the support of other northerners as well as the Federalists, who decided that they had no chance with a candidate of their own.

Madison's followers insisted that the president could not be held responsible for every defeat in the field and that Clinton was a turncoat who had forged a corrupt bargain with the Federalists. Clinton's followers argued that Virginia had had the presidency long enough and that their candidate was a bold and energetic leader who understood the needs of commerce and was friendly to the navy. Clinton was portrayed in prowar states as a man who would shorten the war by prosecuting it more vigorously and in antiwar states as one who would end the war by negotiating with the enemy.

The means of choosing presidential electors varied from state to state. Half chose their electors by popular vote; the rest left the choice up to the legislature. There was no national election day before 1848, which meant that each state was free to follow its own timetable. The results drifted in over a two-month period in late 1812. The voting followed the same sectional pattern as the vote on the declaration of war, with Madison winning the South and West and Clinton the North. The key was Pennsylvania, which enjoyed a booming prosperity fed by large wartime contracts and a surge in imports that came when merchants raced to get their property home after the declaration of war. The Keystone State cast its twenty-five electoral votes

De Witt Clinton (1769–1828), a gifted New York leader, was narrowly defeated when he challenged President Madison in the election of 1812. (Library of Congress)

for Madison, which gave him 128 to Clinton's 89. In 1808, by contrast, Madison had defeated a Federalist opponent by a margin of 122 to 47.

The Republicans also lost ground in the congressional and state elections. The seats they held in the House fell from 75 to 63 percent and in the Senate from 82 to 78 percent. In the elections of 1814 they did not fare much better. Although their strength in the House rose slightly to 65 percent, their strength in the Senate slid to 67 percent. Their losses in state elections were greater. They controlled fourteen of seventeen states in 1811, but by 1813 they controlled only eleven of eighteen. The Federalists had made steady gains and by 1813 controlled all five New England states.

Although the Republicans retained control of the federal government, the election results suggested that there was considerable doubt about the wisdom of the war and the way that it was being managed. Federalists profited from the discontent, registering their most impressive electoral gains since the 1790s.

The Army and Navy

The administration had a persistent problem throughout the war raising the troops that it needed. Congress pushed the authorized level of the army from 10,000 troops in early 1812 to 62,500 by the end of the war, but filling the ranks was no easy task. The nation had no real military tradition, and few people aspired to the life of the common soldier. "Money can usually command men," said a Federalist, "but it will take millions to make soldiers of the happy people of this country—nothing short of a little fortune will induce our farmers or their sons to enter a life which they cordially despise: that of a common soldier."

The only option the government had was to offer ever larger incentives. Army pay was boosted at the start of the war, but the real key was the enlistment bounty, which soared from $12 in 1811 to $124 and 320 acres of land by the end of the war. This was a princely sum, more than most unskilled laborers (who earned $10 to $20 a month) could earn in two years and probably the equivalent of $30,000 today. The incentives pushed troop strength from 12,000 at the beginning of the war to 45,000 at the end, but enlistments always lagged behind need, and those who joined the army needed training and combat experience to become effective soldiers.

To meet its growing need for men, the administration in 1814 recommended that Congress authorize the conscription of militia into the U.S. Army. This proposal went down hard among Republicans and elicited fierce opposition from Federalists in New England. Daniel Webster, who was at the dawn of a long career, urged the New England states to nullify the law—"to interpose between their citizens and arbitrary power." In the face of this opposition, Congress dropped the proposal, and the administration had to fall back on voluntary enlistments.

Defining the navy's role in the war also generated dissension. Initially, most Republicans were against naval expansion, believing that it would be costly and wasteful because any U.S. fleet would be swallowed up by the Royal Navy early in the war. With the unexpected naval victories in 1812, however, many Republicans had a change of heart. In the flush of excitement, Congress authorized four ships-of-the-line, six heavy frigates, and six sloops. Congress later added twenty schooners, mainly for commerce raiding. Although few of these ships were completed before the end of the war, they indicated a commitment to making the nation a naval power.

There was far less opposition to privateering because it was based on private enterprise and thus relied on private financing. As privateers had to shoulder more of the war at sea in the later stages of the war, Congress did what it could to stimulate the practice, lowering the duties on prize goods and offering bounties for the destruction of enemy ships and the capture of enemy seamen. Whether American privateers actually had an impact on the outcome of the war is unclear, but there is no denying that they menaced British trade around the world, driving up insurance rates and exasperating British merchants who were accustomed to treating the sea as their domain.

Congress was more reluctant to devote money to coastal fortifications. This was a critical issue because most of the nation's big cities were on the maritime frontier and thus vulnerable to assault via the sea. Everyone understood that a truly comprehensive system of coastal fortifications would be prohibitively expensive, and some Republicans openly called for abandoning the cities to their fate. In the end, Congress appropriated $1 million for coastal forts, far less than needed. Most cities had to finance their own defense works and rely heavily on militia when enemy warships threatened, an expedient that was both costly and disruptive.

Wartime Finance

Far more divisive was the issue of wartime finance. Before the war Secretary of the Treasury Albert Gallatin had developed a plan of war finance that called for paying for the regular operations of the government (including interest on the national debt) with tax revenue while paying for the cost of the war with loans. With interest on the national debt rising and revenue from trade likely to decline, the plan could only work if Congress authorized new taxes. In January 1812 Gallatin sent the House of Representatives his plan, which called for doubling the taxes on trade and resurrecting the internal duties that had contributed to the defeat of the Federalists in the election of 1800.

Gallatin's request for new taxes created an uproar among congressional Republicans, many of whom feared that the taxes would render their party and the war unpopular. One Republican accused Gallatin of trying "to chill the war spirit," and a Republican newspaper insisted that his aim was to *"frighten the War Hawks"* and *"blow up the cabinet."* Although the House ultimately endorsed Gallatin's plan, it refused to consider any additional taxes until after war was declared, and some Republicans continued to assure their constituents that the war could be won without any new taxes.

After war was declared, Republicans in Congress turned their attention to finance, but while they agreed to double the taxes on trade, they refused to enact the internal taxes that they had endorsed only a few months before. According to a Virginia Federalist, "it was admitted by the ruling party in debate that to impose them now would endanger their success at the next election."

Federalists bitterly protested, claiming that Republicans were imposing new taxes on the North (where most imported goods were consumed) while exempting the South and West. "Is it just and fair," asked a New York Federalist, "to . . . impose so much of the burden of the war upon the people of the northern and eastern states, the majority of whom are known to be opposed to it?"

Republicans turned a deaf ear to these protests and instead met the revenue shortfall by relying on loans and interest-bearing Treasury notes. Not until a year into the war did Congress adopt the internal taxes that Gallatin had said were necessary. A second round of internal taxes was enacted near the end of the war. Together these taxes constituted the most comprehensive system of internal taxes adopted before the Civil War, far more sweeping than the taxes that the Federalists had adopted in the 1790s.

As comprehensive as the Republican tax program was, it was delayed too long to prevent the collapse of public credit in the summer of 1814. The administration was unable to float another war loan that year, and only the neediest of contractors would accept Treasury notes. As a result, the government could not pay its bills or secure the supplies that it needed. It even defaulted on the national debt because it did not have enough gold or silver to make interest payments. For all practical purposes, public credit was extinct, and the government was bankrupt.

The nation's financial woes were further compounded in the summer of 1814 by the suspension of specie payments. The British invasion of the Chesapeake in August created a run on local banks, which responded by refusing to redeem in gold the notes that they had issued. Other banks in the middle and southern states followed suit, and so did those in the West. Once the banks went off a specie-paying basis, they no longer honored one another's notes. The Treasury found that it was accumulating balances in some banks while running out of money in others, and there was no way to rectify the situation by moving money around the country. The suspension of specie payments also cost the Treasury money because it had little choice but to accept depreciated bank paper to meet tax obligations or the fulfillment of loan contracts.

The nation's finances had become so chaotic that by late 1814 the Treasury department was calling for the creation of a national bank. Historically, most Republicans had opposed a national bank, and they had refused to renew the charter of the First National Bank when it had expired in 1811. But as the nation's finances deteriorated, some Republicans had a change of heart. There was no agreement, however, about how a new national bank should be structured or how closely it should be tied to the government. Without a consensus, the proposal for a bank floundered, and news of peace finally killed it.

Trade Restrictions and Enemy Trade

Another divisive issue that Republicans had to deal with was trade restrictions. Before the war the restrictive system had been portrayed as an alternative to armed conflict, as a peaceful means of upholding the nation's rights without resorting to hostilities. Most Republicans, however, showed no interest in giving up the system after war had been declared. As Jefferson's secretary of state, Madison had been the chief architect of the restrictive system, and the war in no way dampened his ardor for using trade as an instrument of foreign policy. Even some of the War Hawks shared his commitment. Six months into the war, Henry Clay conceded that the Republic might be defeated in battle. "But if you cling to the restrictive system," he insisted, "it is incessantly working in your favor," and "if persisted in, the restrictive system, aiding the war, would break down the present [British] ministry, and lead to a consequent honorable peace."

Other Republicans, however, made a bid to jettison the restrictive system soon after war was declared. Spearheading this drive were three South Carolina War Hawks: John C. Calhoun, William Lowndes, and Landon Cheves. According to Cheves, the restrictive system "puts out one eye of your enemy, but it puts out both your own. It exhausts the purse, it exhausts the spirit, and paralyzes the sword of the nation." The ninety-day embargo and non-exportation act that had been adopted in April 1812 were due to expire in July, and Cheves wanted to repeal the non-importation act of 1811 as well, but Congress demurred. This showed that the Republican majority was determined to use trade restrictions as well as armed force to bring the British to terms.

Having disposed of this problem, Congress turned to the closely related but complex issue of regulating trade with the enemy. In spite of widespread support for continuing the restrictive system, there were many Americans, merchants and farmers alike, who opposed any additional restrictions that might limit their wartime economic opportunities. Jefferson, for one, whose own finances were becoming increasingly unmanageable, needed all the revenue that he could get from the commodities that he produced. He told Madison that maintaining agricultural prosperity was vital to the success of the war policy. "To keep open sufficient markets," he said, "is the very first object towards maintaining the popularity of the war."

Other Republicans agreed, and in the summer of 1812 Congress passed a limited enemy trade act that prohibited any trade with British ports but did not bar American merchants from using British licenses to trade with non-British ports. This assured the continued shipment of American provisions to the British army serving in the Spanish Peninsula. The export of American flour to this region had mushroomed from 105,000 barrels in 1809 to 939,000 barrels in 1812. This trade was vital to the success of British arms on the Continent and provided a steady stream of income to American merchants and farmers seeking profit in an uncertain world.

Although the non-importation and enemy trade acts should have prevented any direct trade with the British, the administration found it nearly impossible to enforce these measures. On every frontier—along the Canadian border, on the Atlantic coast, and on the Gulf Coast—there was extensive trade with the enemy, and customs agents as well as army and navy officials seemed powerless to stop it.

The most extensive trade was on the northern frontier, and it steadily increased during the war to meet the needs of the growing British army there. The traffic was carried overland, via inland waterways, and by the sea. "From the St. Lawrence to the ocean," reported an U.S. Army officer in 1814, "an open disregard prevails for the laws prohibiting intercourse with the enemy." As a result of this trade, British troops feasted on American provisions. "Two-thirds of the army in Canada," boasted Sir George Prevost in August 1814, "are at this moment eating beef provided by American contractors."

No less alarming was the trade with British warships off the Atlantic coast. "The fact is notorious," the Lexington *Reporter* declared, "that the very squadrons of the enemy now annoying our coast . . . derive their supplies from the very country which is the theater of their atrocities." Admiralty procurers paid for provisions in cash, and there was no shortage of Americans willing to supply their needs. The Chesapeake Bay, Long Island Sound, and Vineyard Sound teemed with tiny coasters ferrying supplies to British warships. Some sixty vessels were engaged in this traffic in Long Island Sound alone. Although most of the trade was clandestine, the harbor at Provincetown, Massachusetts, on the tip of Cape Cod was openly frequented by British warships seeking supplies or refuge from Atlantic storms. According to one report, small coasters and fishing vessels regularly carried "fresh beef, vegetables, and in fact all kind of supplies" to these ships.

Amelia Island, a Spanish possession at the mouth of St. Marys River in Florida, was an important entrepôt for the exchange of southern produce for British manufactured goods. Shortly before the war, Gallatin received reports "that British goods to an immense amount have been imported into Amelia Island, with the view of smuggling the same into the United States."

There was also considerable illicit trade on the Gulf Coast. The Baratarian pirates had established a base on Grand Terre Island in southern Louisiana, and from there they smuggled goods—British and non-British alike—into New Orleans. The pirates operated openly and were welcomed by local merchants because the trade was so lucrative. "I will not dissemble," the secretary of the treasury told the New Orleans customs collector in 1813, "that whilst the inhabitants of Louisiana continue to countenance this illegal commerce and the courts of justice forbear to enforce the laws against the offenders, little or no benefit can be expected to result from the best concerted measures."

The illegal trade knew no political or social barriers. Federalists and Republicans alike profited from the trade, local and state officials were often complicit, and even federal officials sometimes looked the other way. The trade gave a boost to local economies, a boost that was sorely needed because even though the middle and western states prospered during the war (mainly from war contracts) New England and the South suffered. British officials were surprised at how eager Americans were to supply their needs. "Self, the great ruling principle," said one Royal Navy officer, is "more powerful with Yankees than any people I ever saw."

President Madison repeatedly asked Congress for more trade restrictions, both to put economic pressure on Great Britain and to deny British forces in North America the provisions that sustained them, but most of his proposals failed in one house or the other. When Madison learned in early 1813 of a British order directing officials in the West Indies to favor antiwar New England with the licenses they issued, he asked Congress to outlaw the use of all such licenses. Congress refused to act until the summer of 1813 and only after a federal court had ruled in the *Julia* case that an American ship carrying an enemy license was a legitimate prize of war.

By the summer of 1813 Madison had become so alarmed by the growing trade with the enemy that he asked Congress for an embargo on all American exports. Madison's proposal was treated roughly in both houses and never became law. The president was dismayed, insisting that such a ban would have "driven the enemy out of Canada, expelled him from our waters, and forced him to retire from Spain and Portugal." Madison renewed his plea for an embargo at the end of 1813, and by then trade with the enemy had become such a public scandal that Congress complied. The embargo of 1813 was more sweeping than any previous trade restriction. It prohibited American ships from leaving port, banned the export of all goods and commodities, and gave extensive powers to government officials to enforce the measure.

Whatever satisfaction the president took from the embargo was short-lived because at the end of 1813 news arrived of Napoleon's defeat at Leipzig. This opened all of northern Europe to British trade and thus deprived American trade restrictions of their coercive power. There were growing calls to end the restrictive system, and by the spring of 1814 Madison himself had had enough. In a message to Congress on March 31 that stunned nearly everyone, the president asked for the repeal of the embargo and non-importation act. Although die-hard restrictionists fought a rearguard action, Congress repealed both measures.

Since trade with the enemy, especially across the northern frontier, continued to be a problem, Congress in early 1815 adopted a new and sweeping enemy trade act that gave government officials extensive powers to combat the traffic. This law never received a fair test, however, because it expired when peace was restored two weeks later. Whether it would have worked may be doubted. The enforcement machinery of the Treasury Department, even when aided by the army and navy, remained primitive, and people living on the frontiers showed a remarkable determination and ingenuity to keep profitable avenues of trade open.

Prisoners of War

Another problem that the administration had to deal with was how to manage prisoners of war. Although there was no international treaty on the subject, each side professed to favor humane treatment. The precedents, however, were vague and far from binding, and in sharp contrast to modern practice, both sides treated common seamen as combatants. American prisoners were particularly unhappy with the terms of their imprisonment, complaining of crowded, cold, and dirty housing, foul rations, and occasionally of physical abuse.

Officers were considered gentlemen and thus received special treatment. Most were given the freedom of a town or larger area and occasionally sent home on an extended parole with the understanding that they not return to the field until exchanged. Members of the militia were also sometimes sent home because they were considered part-time soldiers. Enlisted men, on the other hand, were usually confined until exchanged.

The United States took close to 20,000 prisoners during the war, but many were seamen taken by privateers. Most of the seamen as well as others taken on land or at sea were immediately released or paroled. Hence, accommodations in the United States had to be found for fewer than 10,000 prisoners. The administration favored state or local jails near (but not too near) the northern frontier, particularly in Massachusetts and Kentucky. It also employed unoccupied buildings in cities and even a few prison ships on the Atlantic seaboard.

Great Britain also took around 20,000 prisoners, most of whom were privateersmen. Among those imprisoned were American seamen trapped in Great Britain during the war as well as those who had been serving in the Royal Navy and asked to be excused when the war began. To house their prisoners, the British used jails and prison ships in British ports scattered around the Atlantic. The two largest prisons were on Melville Island in Halifax Harbor (which housed over 8,000 prisoners) and Dartmoor in southeastern England (which was home to 6,500).

In principle, all enlisted men, whether taken on land or at sea, were treated the same. Although the United States adhered to this principle, the British did not. To deter privateering, the British refused to exchange anyone taken from a privateer carrying fewer than fourteen guns. The British also had a reputation for making life hard on maritime prisoners in the hope of inducing them to volunteer for service in the chronically shorthanded Royal Navy.

Initially both sides adopted liberal parole and exchange policies on the northern frontier, but this changed when a dispute arose over the treatment of prisoners of doubtful nationality. In the Battle of Queenston Heights, fought in October 1812, the British took a large number of prisoners, including twenty-three who had been born in the British Isles. Most of these were Irishmen who had become naturalized Americans or had long resided in the United States. Royal officials, however, considered them traitors, and they were clamped in irons and shipped to England to be tried for treason.

The United States responded by ordering twenty-three British prisoners held in close confinement as hostages. The British retaliated by confining forty-six American officers and non-commissioned officers, and American officials followed suit. Retaliation continued on both sides until by early 1814, all officers held as prisoners in North America by either side were in close confinement with the threat of retaliatory execution hanging over their heads.

London officials were livid over the threat of American retaliation, and British newspapers bitterly denounced the American threat. The issue stirred up domestic controversy in United States because some Federalists took Britain's side in the dispute. The Federalist-controlled Maryland House of Delegates protested against the "system of sanguinary retaliation" which jeopardized American prisoners to protect "British traitors," and Massachusetts barred prisoners of war from its facilities. In addition, someone, probably a Federalist, helped British officers escape from a jail in Worcester, Massachusetts.

Fortunately, good sense ultimately prevailed in Great Britain, and the issue was defused. The British did not take any action against the original twenty-three prisoners and all those held in close confinement on both sides were eventually released. There were several other cases in which the British threatened to prosecute American prisoners born in the British Isles, but in each case the threat of U.S. retaliation forced them to relent.

Federalist Opposition

The most persistent and vexing domestic problem that the administration faced during the war was Federalist opposition. The opposition was especially unrelenting in New England, and this weighed heavily on the president in the final stages of the war. "You are not mistaken," he told a friend in November 1814, "in viewing the conduct of the eastern states as the source of our greatest difficulties in carrying on the war."

Ever since 1806, Federalists had been sharply critical of Republican foreign policy. They had denounced the loss of the Monroe–Pinkney Treaty in 1807 and the embargo and the other trade restrictions that had followed. There was an element of truth in their criticisms, which made them all the more difficult for Republicans to bear. One of the reasons that Republicans had gone to war in 1812 was to silence their domestic critics. A state of war, they assumed, would force everyone, even Federalists, to rally to the flag. "A declaration of war," said New Hampshire Republican William Plumer, "must necessarily produce a great change in public opinion and the state of parties—British partisans must then either close their lips in silence or abscond."

As the nation inched toward war in early 1812, Republicans ominously hinted at what Federalists might expect if they did not rally to the cause. Once war is declared, said Tennessee War Hawk Felix Grundy in the halls of Congress, the only question would be "are you for your country or against it." Whenever that decision is made, echoed the semi-official Washington *National Intelligencer*, "he that is not for us must be considered as against us and treated accordingly."

Many of the pleas carried the threat of violence. Even Thomas Jefferson did not escape the growing spirit of intolerance. "The Federalists," he told the president shortly after the declaration of war, " . . . are poor devils here, not worthy of notice. A barrel of tar to each state south of the Potomac will keep all in order, and that will be freely contributed without troubling government. To the north they will give you more trouble. You may there have to apply the rougher drastic of . . . hemp and confiscation." Perhaps Jefferson was speaking in jest, but other Republicans took the matter more seriously. Many agreed with the Boston *Yankee* that the war offered a way to "insure peace at home, if not with the world."

Republican intolerance exploded into violence in the early months of the war. In Baltimore a series of vicious prowar riots destroyed the offices of a Federalist newspaper and left one Federalist (James M. Lingan) dead and two others (editor Alexander C. Hanson and "Light-Horse" Harry Lee—the father of Robert E. Lee) with crippling injuries from which they never recovered. Republican mobs drove another Federalist newspaper out of business in Savannah, Georgia, and assaulted a Federalist editor in Norristown, Pennsylvania. Other Federalist editors in the middle or southern states were warned to tone down their opposition or risk a similar fate. "The war," concluded a Federalist newspaper in Connecticut, "pretendedly for the freedom of the seas, is valiantly waged against the freedom of the press."

Although some Federalists in the middle and southern states had considered supporting the war, or at least remaining silent, Republican violence gave them pause. They were also disheartened by other decisions made at the beginning of the war: the refusal to limit the war to the high seas and to include France in the reprisals, the failure to repeal the restrictive system, and the discriminatory tax policy adopted. Convinced that the war was a partisan war designed to further the interests of the ruling party, Federalists everywhere denounced the contest as unnecessary, unwise, and unjust. "Whether we consider our agriculture, our commerce, our monied systems, or our internal safety," concluded a Federalist newspaper in Virginia, "nothing but disaster can result from it."

The best way to bring the war to a speedy end, most Federalists agreed, was to oppose it. The declaration of war was like any other bad law, said Harrison Gray Otis of Massachusetts. "It must be obeyed but its mischief may be and ought to be freely discussed and all due means taken to procure its repeal." In Congress Federalists voted as a bloc on all war legislation. They unanimously opposed the declaration of war in June 1812, and thereafter they voted against almost every proposal to raise men or money, foster privateering, or restrict trade with the enemy. The only measures they supported were those they considered sound long-term investments in defense—mainly bills to increase the navy or build coastal fortifications.

Federalists in New England went further. They wrote, spoke, and preached against the war, discouraged enlistments in the army and subscriptions to the war loans, and denounced all who supported the war and worked for their defeat at the polls. For some in New England, supporting such an unjust war was positively sinful. "Each man who volunteers his services in such a cause," said a Massachusetts preacher, "or loans his money for its support, or by his conversation, his writings, or any other mode of influence, encourages its prosecution . . . loads his conscience with the blackest crimes."

Because they were the dominant party in New England, Federalists did not have to worry about being persecuted, and they could use the machinery of state and local government to obstruct the war effort. In Hartford, Connecticut, Federalists sought to curtail loud demonstrations by army recruiters by adopting city ordinances that restricted public music and parades. In New Bedford, Massachusetts, Federalists denounced privateering and voted to quarantine all arriving privateers for forty days, ostensibly to control epidemic disease but actually to protest the war.

New England Federalists made their opposition felt in other ways. After a Republican newspaper chided Federalists in Massachusetts for celebrating naval victories in a war they opposed, the Federalist-controlled state senate adopted a resolution declaring that "in a war like the present . . . it is not becoming [of] a moral and religious people to express any approbation of military and naval exploits which are not immediately connected with the defense of our seacoast and soil."

New England's Defense Problem

The most persistent source of controversy between the federal government and New England was over the deployment and control of the militia. This was no small matter because the militia units in New England were among the best in the nation. They were an important source of local pride and tradition, and most Federalists saw the militia as their best if not their only means of defense.

The first clash occurred in 1812 shortly after the declaration of war. The regulars in the coastal fortifications in the region had been ordered to the northern frontier, and the War Department asked the governors of Massachusetts, Connecticut, and Rhode Island to call out militia to replace them. All three governors refused, claiming that there was no imminent danger and that they could not permit their militia to serve under ranking regular army officers in charge of each fort anyway. This defiance was a way of publicizing their opposition to the war, but it also reflected a fear that any militia serving under regular officers might be ordered to Canada, leaving the region defenseless.

When the British actually threatened, the New England governors were willing to call out their militia. They also tried to resolve the command problem but without much success. Matters came to a head in the summer of 1814 when the British targeted the New England coastline, necessitating calling out numerous units of citizen soldiers. When efforts to paper over the command problem failed, the troops were placed exclusively under state officers, and the federal government responded by cutting off supplies and pay. This meant that in the final months of the war, Massachusetts, Connecticut, and Rhode Island had to fund local defense measures.

These costs steadily mounted, eventually totaling $850,000 in Massachusetts, $150,000 in Connecticut, and $50,000 in Rhode Island. Raising money to meet these costs was no easy matter. New taxes were especially unwelcome because the federal burden was large and still growing at a time when New England was in the throes of a wartime depression. Nor could local banks help out. The suspension of specie payments elsewhere in the Union had forced the banks in New England to retrench in order to hold on to their cash reserves. No one knew when the war would end, and hence the growing cash crunch that the states faced was a source of considerable alarm.

The Hartford Convention

The defense problem was New England's chief grievance in 1814, but it was only a symptom of a broader Federalist disillusionment with more than a decade of Republican rule. No less disheartening, Federalists could see little prospect of winning control of the national government so that they might effect change. In spite of their wartime losses, the Republicans remained firmly in control of the national government, and there was little prospect of dislodging them anytime soon. The Louisiana Purchase in 1803 had brought vast new territories under U.S. control, and the flood of immigrants into the West (which was slowed but not halted by the war) promised to populate these territories with Republican voters and guarantee that they would eventually join the Union as Republican states.

Traditionally, Americans had met a crisis by calling a convention to consider what action to take. The Albany Congress (1754), the Stamp Act Congress (1765), the

First Continental Congress (1774), and the Philadelphia Constitutional Convention (1787) were all summoned to deal with a crisis. To address the crisis they faced in 1814, New England Federalists summoned the Hartford Convention.

The Hartford Convention met from December 15, 1814, to January 5, 1815, and like many deliberative bodies in those days, it met in secret. Although there was talk in some Federalist newspapers about seeking a separate peace and withdrawing from the Union, the delegates to the Hartford Convention were moderates determined to avoid any precipitous action. The report of the convention, which was largely the work of Harrison Gray Otis, reflected this moderation.

About half of the report was devoted to immediate issues related to the war: the defense problem and the danger that Congress might resort to conscription or the enlistment of minors. To finance local defense measures, the report recommended that the state governments seek authority from the national government to use federal tax money collected within their borders. To deal with unconstitutional measures for raising troops, the report (in its only radical proposal) recommended nullification, claiming that it was the duty of a state "to interpose its authority" to protect its citizens.

This cartoon of the Hartford Convention depicts the King of England inviting Harrison Gray Otis to bring the New England states into the British Empire. The three delegates considering the "leap" represent Massachusetts, Connecticut, and Rhode Island. Governor Caleb Strong below prays for a successful leap so that he can join the British aristocracy as Lord Essex. (Etching by William Charles. Library of Congress)

The rest of the report was devoted to long-term problems. To remedy these, the report called for a series of amendments to the U.S. Constitution. These would require a two-thirds vote in Congress to declare war, limit trade, or admit new states to the Union; limit embargoes to sixty days; end the rule that counted three-fifths of slaves for apportioning representation in Congress; bar naturalized citizens from federal office; limit presidents to a single term; and prohibit the election of the president from the same state twice in a row.

These amendments represented a catalogue of New England's grievances during the Republican ascendancy. They targeted the restrictive system and war; the overrepresentation of white southerners in Congress; the growing political power of the West; the influence of foreign-born officeholders (like Swiss-born Albert Gallatin); and Virginia's domination of the presidency. Federalists believed that the adoption of these amendments would restore sectional balance and prevent a renewal of those Republican policies that they considered most harmful to New England and the nation.

Massachusetts and Connecticut approved the amendments and sent emissaries to Washington to secure federal tax money for defense measures. On their way they learned of Jackson's victory at New Orleans, and just as they reached the capital, news of the peace treaty arrived. The envoys were the butt of much Republican humor, and nothing came of their mission.

The Hartford Convention was the climax of Federalist opposition to the War of 1812. Although it represented a triumph for moderation, few people remembered it that way in the rush of events at the end of the war. Instead, the Hartford Convention became a synonym for treason, and all of the shortcomings of the war were blamed on the Federalists. People forgot that both parties were involved in the inner war and that Republicans no less than Federalists deserved a share of the blame for the misfortunes of the war.

Chapter 6
───────────

The Peace of Christmas Eve

On the battlefield, the record of the United States during the War of 1812 was mixed. There were some shining moments—the naval victories on the northern lakes and the high seas, the success in the West at the Thames and Horseshoe Bend, the Army's fine showing at Chippawa, Lundy's Lane, and Fort Erie on the Niagara, the defense of Fort McHenry in the Chesapeake, and Jackson's great victory at New Orleans. But there were also plenty of defeats and failures. The nation never conquered Canada, it was unable to defend against British depredations on the Atlantic Coast, and it never found a way to lessen the crushing impact of the British blockade. Worst of all, there was the humiliating and demoralizing occupation of Washington and the burning of the public buildings there.

In the peace negotiations, however, the nation's record was much better, not because of what American diplomats won but because of what they avoided losing. No single campaign in the field loomed as large as these negotiations. It was here—in Ghent (in modern-day Belgium) rather than on the battlefield—that the United States consistently outmaneuvered the enemy, and it was here that Americans could claim their most significant victory in the war.

Was the Declaration of War a Bluff?

American success at the negotiating table was fitting because it was here that many Republicans expected to win the war. Some Republicans—the "scarecrow" party—had supported war preparations in 1811–1812 in the hope that the prospect of war alone would be enough to win concessions from the British. When this failed, some voted for the declaration of war for the same reason. Although most

Republicans believed that the conquest of Canada would be a mere matter of marching, many hoped that no marching would be necessary, that the declaration of war itself would shock the British into concessions. In this sense, the declaration of war was a kind of bluff designed to force the British to take American demands seriously.

That President Madison himself harbored these views is suggested by the haste with which he sent out peace feelers. "The sword was scarcely out of the scabbard," he said, "before the enemy was apprised of the reasonable terms on which it would be resheathed." Madison spelled out American peace terms to the departing British minister, Augustus J. Foster, and Secretary of State James Monroe urged Foster to work for peace.

The administration also pursued peace through Jonathan Russell, America's diplomatic representative in London. On June 26, barely a week after the declaration of war, the State Department authorized Russell to sign an armistice if the British would give up the Orders-in-Council and impressment. By the time Russell made this offer in late August, the Orders-in-Council had already been repealed. That meant that impressment was the only issue that stood in the way of peace.

The British, however, showed no interest in the American offer. Having made one important concession—the repeal of the Orders—they were in no mood to make another, certainly not on an issue that could threaten their mastery of the sea. With the war only a few weeks old, Britain's foreign secretary, Lord Castlereagh, was surprised that the United States was so eager for peace. "If the American government was so anxious *to get rid of the war,*" he told Russell, "it would have an opportunity of doing so on learning of the revocation of the Orders-in-Council."

The British assumed that the repeal of the Orders would lead to peace. For years, British restrictions on neutral trade had been the overriding issue in Anglo-American relations, while impressment had not been a major issue since the loss of the Monroe-Pinkney Treaty and the eruption of the *Chesapeake* affair in 1807. Convinced that peace was likely, the British authorized Sir George Prevost in Canada to propose a cease-fire. The result was an armistice signed by Prevost's agent and Major General Henry Dearborn in August 1812. But the U.S. government repudiated the agreement because it did not provide for an end to impressment.

Thus, even though both sides were interested in peace, the negotiations in the summer of 1812 failed. The United States went ahead with its ill-fated invasion of Canada, and the British reluctantly accepted the state of war. But Great Britain waited until October 13—ten weeks after receiving news of the declaration of war—before authorizing general reprisals against the United States and another three months—until January 9, 1813—before issuing a state paper justifying their position on the maritime issues that had caused the war.

The Russian Mediation Offer

In March 1813, with the war less than nine months old, Andrei Dashkov, the Russian minister in Washington, offered the services of his government as a mediator. The Russians had several reasons for acting. They did not want to see their British allies diverting any military and naval resources from the war on the Continent to North America, and they were eager to regain access to tropical produce from the West Indies that American ships normally brought to the Baltic. This trade had come to an abrupt halt with the outbreak of the War of 1812 and would not likely resume until peace was restored.

The administration welcomed the Russian offer. Russia had long championed neutral rights, and there was every reason to expect that it would take a favorable view of the American position on the issue. "There is not a single [maritime] interest," Monroe commented, "in which Russia and the other Baltic powers may not be considered as having common interest with the United States."

American officials were anxious for peace for several reasons. The campaign of 1812 had not gone well, Federalist opposition remained adamant, and the financial situation of the Republic was already deteriorating. In addition, the news from the Continent was not encouraging. After losing an army in Russia, Napoleon appeared to be on the run. With the allies in the ascendant, there was good reason to fear that Napoleon might be defeated, and this would leave the United States in the field alone against Great Britain. The administration was eager to liquidate the war in the New World while Britain was still tied up in the Old.

Without waiting for Britain's response, Madison chose three peace commissioners and sent them to Europe. Albert Gallatin was chosen to head the mission. He was eager to shed his duties at the Treasury Department and had grown weary of the bitter attacks he was subjected to by both parties in Congress. He was joined by John Quincy Adams, who was serving as U.S. minister to Russia, and James A. Bayard, a moderate Delaware Federalist. The Senate rejected Gallatin's nomination because Madison insisted on keeping him as head of the Treasury Department, but by then the three envoys were already in Europe.

The administration drew up instructions to guide the commissioners that called for a broad range of concessions on the maritime issues and even suggested that the British would be wise to surrender Canada to avoid future conflict. But only one demand was a *sine qua non*—that is, a point deemed essential to any agreement—and that was an end to impressment.

Gallatin and Bayard joined Adams in St. Petersburg in July 1813. There they attended an unending round of parties waiting for Britain's official response to the mediation offer. In fact, the British had already rejected the offer. They had no desire, said Castlereagh, to allow the United States "to mix directly or indirectly her maritime interests with those of another state"—certainly not with those of a great inland power likely to favor a broad definition of neutral rights. The Russians were reluctant to admit it, but their mediation offer was dead.

The British Counteroffer

Although the British rejected Russia's offer, they felt obliged to make a counteroffer to show their peaceful intentions. Hence in a message to Monroe dated November 4, 1813, Castlereagh proposed direct talks. He made it clear, however, that Britain would surrender none of its maritime rights, which meant there was little prospect for any concessions on the impressment issue.

Castlereagh's letter reached Washington on a truce ship at the end of 1813. President Madison accepted the British offer and appointed four men to serve on the U.S. negotiating team. John Quincy Adams was chosen to head the delegation. The other members were Bayard, Kentucky War Hawk Henry Clay, and Jonathan Russell, who had conducted the armistice negotiations in London in 1812. When Madison learned that Gallatin was still in Europe, he was added to the commission. This time the president mollified the Senate by appointing a new secretary of the treasury.

The American delegation was exceptionally strong. Four of the envoys already had distinguished themselves in public life, and Adams and Clay still had long and important careers ahead of them. Only Russell would never achieve any great distinction. With such a strong delegation, differences of opinion were inevitable. Clay and Adams frequently clashed, though usually on minor issues. "Upon almost all the important questions," Adams later said, "we have been unanimous."

The British waited until May 1814 to appoint their own delegation. By then the war in Europe was over, which put the British in a strong bargaining position. Britain's top officials continued to focus on the Continent, preparing for a conference at Vienna that would hammer out a peace settlement for Europe. The negotiating team sent to Ghent was composed of lesser lights. Heading the delegation was Lord Gambier, a veteran naval officer who was expected to protect Britain's maritime rights. Also on the delegation were Dr. William Adams, an Admiralty lawyer, and Henry Goulburn, an undersecretary in the Colonial Office. Goulburn was the most ambitious and energetic of the three, and he took the lead in the negotiations.

The British envoys were slow to depart for Ghent because officials in London hoped that success in the current campaign would enhance their bargaining power. Although Liverpool and Castlereagh remained levelheaded and cool, the mood throughout the realm was vindictive. "War with America, and most inveterate war," said a friendly Englishman, "is in the mouth of almost everyone you meet in this wise and thinking nation."

American leaders hoped that the Great Powers on the Continent would serve as a counterpoise to British strength and have a moderating influence on British policy, but no one in Europe had any taste for meddling in the war or antagonizing Great Britain. Still, everyone—the British included—recognized that the American war limited Britain's freedom of action on the Continent, and gradually sympathy for the United States increased. The Republic profited from this sympathy. Despite British protests, French officials continued to admit American privateers to French ports even though France was now at peace with Great Britain.

Britain's Peace Terms

The peace negotiations were originally planned for Gothenburg, Sweden, but with the war in Europe now over, Ghent was substituted because it provided quicker access to both capitals. The negotiations lasted from August 8 to December 24, 1814, far longer than anyone anticipated but not as long as the Congress of Vienna, whose deliberations dragged on from September 15, 1814, to June 9, 1815.

On the eve of the negotiations, the American envoys were still bound to insist on an end to impressment, but with the British in the ascendant everyone now realized the hopelessness of this demand. Like other U.S. diplomats in this era, the American delegation was prepared to violate its instructions, but this became unnecessary when the administration bowed to reality and dropped the impressment issue. The new instructions reached Ghent just as the negotiations got under way.

With impressment out of the way, the envoys were able to focus on other issues. In the first two weeks of the negotiations, the British laid down their terms. As a *sine qua non* for peace, they insisted that the Indians in the Old Northwest be included in the settlement and that a permanent reservation be established for them. The British also demanded territorial concessions in northern Maine (to facilitate traffic between Quebec and Halifax) and in present-day Minnesota (to assure access to the Mississippi River). In addition, they insisted that the United States unilaterally demilitarize the lakes, removing all warships from those waters and all fortifications from the shores. Finally, the British announced that the American right to fish in Canadian waters and dry the catch on Canadian shores would be annulled unless the United States offered an equivalent concession.

The British demands were based on several considerations, but uppermost was the desire to win security for Canada and Britain's Indian allies. No one thought that this would be the last Anglo-American war, nor did anyone doubt that the United States would gain in population and power and would continue to retain a keen interest in territorial expansion. The British needed to find some way to protect their subjects in North America from future aggression from the south. They were also anxious to protect their Indian allies, whom they had abandoned in the Peace of 1783 and the Jay Treaty of 1794.

As a boundary for the Indian reservation, the British suggested that the line established by the Treaty of Greenville in 1795 might serve as a starting point though subject to "such modifications as might be agreed upon." This treaty has been superseded by others that opened additional lands to American settlers, but if resurrected, it would have secured to the Indians about a third of Ohio, half of Minnesota, and almost all of Indiana, Illinois, Michigan, and Wisconsin.

The territory did not, as the American envoys claimed, embrace a third of the land mass of the United States but rather about 250,000 square miles or 15 percent. It was inhabited by close to 45,000 Indians and perhaps 100,000 whites. When asked what would become of the Americans who found themselves on the wrong side of the boundary line, the British envoys replied that "they must shift for themselves"—which meant they would have to abandon their homes and move to the other side of the line.

The British terms need not have surprised anyone since they were anticipated by newspapers on both sides of the Atlantic. The U.S. envoys, however, were stunned. Although aware of the strident anti-American feeling in Great Britain, they had assumed that the British government would be much more moderate.

The U.S. envoys flatly rejected the British terms. "A treaty concluded upon such terms," they said, "would be but an armistice. It cannot be supposed that America would long submit to conditions so injurious and degrading." The Indian reservation was particularly objectionable. It undermined American sovereignty, ran counter to the tradition of national control over the Indians, and threatened the westward movement.

With the talks apparently stalled, the outlook of the American delegation became gloomy. Only Henry Clay saw even a ray of hope. An inveterate gambler, Clay spent his nights at Ghent playing cards, and he suspected that the British might be bluffing, that they would be unwilling to allow the talks to break up over the issues in question. "Such a rupture," he said, "would entirely change the whole character of the war, would unite all parties at home, and would organize a powerful opposition in Great Britain."

Clay's hunch proved correct. Far from being fixed in stone, the British terms were what one scholar has called "a probing operation." Their purpose was to establish a basis for negotiation and to determine what concessions the United States might be willing to make. Even the Indian reservation was not supposed to be a *sine qua non,* although the British envoys misinterpreted their instructions and presented it as one.

The British Retreat

Unwilling to end the negotiations, the British gradually retreated from their demands. Instead of an Indian reservation, the British settled for a provision that simply restored the Indians to their status as of 1811. But most of the tribes had already agreed to other terms with the United States, and the Ghent stipulation was probably too vague to be meaningful anyway. In effect, the British had abandoned their Indian allies again.

Having retreated from their initial terms, the British in October 1814 proposed a new basis for peace: *uti possidetis*. This Latin phrase meant that each side would keep whatever territory it held when the treaty went into effect. If this were agreed to, the United States would retain Fort Amherstburg on the Detroit and Fort Erie on the Niagara, while the British would gain eastern Maine, Mackinac Island, Fort Niagara, and Prairie du Chien.

The British suggested that the agreement be "subject to such modifications as mutual convenience may be found to require." They hoped to get enough of northern Maine to establish the direct connection they wanted between Quebec and Halifax. The other posts might be exchanged so that both nations would recover what they held before the war. The British gave no thought at this time to the fate of New Orleans. Their entire Gulf Coast campaign was all but ignored as they weighed their options in the peace negotiations.

When the United States showed no interest in peace on the basis of *uti possidetis,* the British dropped this proposal just they had their earlier demands. By this time the British no longer counted on developments in the field to strengthen their hand. The reports of the seizure of eastern Maine and the occupation of Washington had buoyed their hopes, but news soon followed that they had been rebuffed at Plattsburgh and Baltimore. Great Britain's counteroffensive in 1814 had not brought the kind of success that officials in London had expected.

Moreover, the mood of the British people was beginning to shift. The shrill attacks on the United States had given way to loud protests against war taxes. "Economy and relief from taxation are not merely the war cry of opposition," conceded one British official, "but they are the real objects to which public attention is turned." After two decades of almost constant warfare, the British people had become war weary.

Another year of warfare in North America was likely to be costly and to weaken Britain's position in Europe. The allies at Vienna were already quarreling among themselves, and British officials were wondering how quickly they could bring troops home from America. "The negotiations at Vienna are not proceeding in the way we could wish," commented the prime minister, Lord Liverpool, "and this consideration itself was deserving of some weight in deciding the question of peace with America."

To strengthen their position at home and in the field, British officials asked the Duke of Wellington, fresh from his victories over the French in the Spanish Peninsula, to take command of the American war. The Iron Duke agreed but was unwilling to leave Europe until the spring and did not expect much from a change in command. "I feel no objection to going to America," he told Liverpool, "though I don't promise to myself much success there." What the British needed in America was "not a general, or general officers and troops, but a naval superiority on the lakes." Without this, there was little hope of success. Given existing circumstances, Wellington concluded, "you have no right . . . to demand any concession of territory from America."

Wellington's opinion was all the cover that British leaders needed to jettison their last territorial demands. The doctrine of *uti possidetis* was discarded and with it any hope of acquiring part of Maine or any other territory. The only issues that remained were U.S. fishing privileges in Canadian waters and the British right to use the Mississippi River. Since both rights were guaranteed by the Treaty of 1783, they were likely to stand or fall together.

Status of the Treaty of 1783

Debate over these issues raised a fundamental question: did the onset of war abrogate all prior treaties? The assumption in Europe was that it did, but no one wanted to reopen issues that had been settled long ago. Hence, European peace treaties typically reaffirmed all prior treaties between the warring nations. In keeping with European practices, the British argued that the onset of war in 1812 had nullified the Treaty of 1783. The American envoys disagreed, claiming that the earlier treaty could never be abrogated, that it enjoyed a special status because it guaranteed U.S. independence.

The debate over the fisheries and the navigation of the Mississippi created a deep division in the U.S. delegation. Clay, representing western interests, wanted to end British navigation of the Mississippi, while Adams, representing the New England fisheries, wanted to continue the fishing privileges. Ultimately, both issues were left out of the treaty, which was a victory for Adams because the British conceded that both privileges continued. This was also a victory for the United States because while the fishing privilege remained lucrative, British fur traders who once had shipped their furs down the Mississippi River to New Orleans were increasingly sending their furs east to Montreal.

The Treaty of Ghent

The envoys spent close to a month hammering the treaty into final form. Their handiwork was completed on December 24 and is known as the Treaty of Ghent or the Peace of Christmas Eve. The treaty was silent on the maritime issues that had caused the war. There was no mention of the Orders-in-Council, impressment, territorial waters, or naval blockades.

The treaty simply restored the *status quo ante bellum*—the state that had existed before the war. This meant that all conquered territory would be returned. Each nation promised to make peace with the Indians and "to restore to such tribes . . . all the possessions, rights, and privileges which they may have enjoyed, or been entitled to" in 1811. Three commissions were established to settle disputed portions of the Canadian-American boundary, and both nations promised to "use their best endeavors" stamp out the slave trade.

The commissioners at Ghent had to decide when the peace treaty would go into effect. In Europe the signing of the treaty normally ended a war, but on three earlier occasions the British had been burned by American attempts to revise a treaty after it had been signed but before it had been ratified. This happened with the Jay Treaty in 1794, a boundary convention in 1803, and the Monroe–Pinkney Treaty in 1806. At Ghent the British made it clear they would settle for nothing less than unconditional ratification. Hence, the treaty provided for hostilities to end only when both sides had ratified it.

Ratification

The Treaty of Ghent reached London in a couple of days, and on December 27, the British government ratified it. Anthony Baker, secretary to the British peace delegation, boarded the truce ship *Favourite* on January 2, 1815, to carry the British instrument of ratification to America. He was joined by Henry Carroll, Clay's personal secretary, who was taking an American copy of the treaty to Washington.

The Treaty of Ghent was signed on Christmas Eve in 1814. Pictured here the two delegation heads, Vice Admiral James Gambier on the left and John Quincy Adams on the right, are shaking hands surrounded by members of their respective delegations. (Lithograph of painting by A. Forestier. Library and Archives of Canada)

The *Favourite* ran into bad weather when it neared the Chesapeake and hence headed north and docked in New York's harbor around 8:00 p.m. on February 11. Carroll made no secret of his mission, and soon the entire city was celebrating. From New York, the news quickly spread in all directions. An express rider carried the news to Boston in a record thirty-two hours. Handbills announcing the treaty soon appeared all over the city. Schools were closed, people left their jobs, and the legislature adjourned. In the boisterous celebration that ensued, bells were rung, buildings were illuminated, troops turned out to fire a salute, and cartmen with the word "peace" on their hats led a procession of sleighs around the city.

As word spread, celebrations like this broke out all over the land. "Grand il-luminations are making throughout the United States," reported one observer. Everywhere the news of peace buoyed the price of war bonds and Treasury notes as well as goods that were normally marketed overseas. The price of war material, by contrast, sagged, while those of scarce imported goods collapsed altogether.

The British were prepared to offer a separate peace to New England if the United States refused to ratify the agreement or insisted on changes in the treaty, but there was no danger of this happening. President Madison received Carroll's copy of the treaty on February 15 and submitted it to the Senate. By a vote of thirty-five to zero, the Senate voted its approval the next day. Madison signed off on the agreement later that day, and with this the war ended. Both sides sent out orders suspending all military and naval operations. At 11:00 p.m. on February 17, Baker, who was now in Washington with the British copy of the treaty, exchanged ratifications with Sec-retary of State James Monroe. With this act, the terms of the treaty became binding on both sides.

The Reaction to Peace

Although everyone in the United States was happy that the war was over, Federalists thought they had a special reason to celebrate. The war, after all, had achieved none of the nation's objectives. The maritime issues were ignored in the peace treaty, and Canada remained in British hands. The terms of the Treaty of Ghent seemed to confirm what Federalists had been saying all along about the futility of the conflict. Many Federalists assumed that once the excitement died down and Americans took a closer look at the treaty, the administration would be discredited and Federalists would reap significant political dividends.

James Robertson, a Philadelphia Federalist, was not so optimistic. The Repub-licans, he predicted, would ignore the causes of the conflict and portray it as "a war on our part of pure self-defense against the designs of the British to reduce us again to [colonial] subjugation." By portraying the war in this light, they could claim that it was a great triumph for the fledgling Republic. "The president," Robertson concluded, "will only have to call it a glorious peace, and the party here will echo it."

Robertson's prediction proved correct. In a message to Congress announcing the end of the war, President Madison congratulated Americans "upon an event which is highly honorable to the nation, and terminates, with peculiar felicity, a campaign signalized by the most brilliant successes." The war, Madison concluded, "has been waged with a success which is the natural result of the wisdom of the legislative councils, of the patriotism of the people, of the public spirit of the militia, and of the valor of the military and naval forces of the country."

All across the nation Republican orators and editors echoed the president's cry. "This second war of independence," crowed the New York *National Advocate*, "has been illustrated by more splendid achievements than the war of the revolution." The nation had attained all of its objectives, added a writer for the Washington *National Intelligencer*. "The administration has succeeded in asserting the principles of God and nature against the encroachments of human ambition and tyranny."

The Republicans exaggerated, for in spite of the victories on land, on the lakes, and at sea, the United States could not in good conscience claim to have won the war. But because of the hard-headed determination shown by its envoys at Ghent, the nation could at least claim that it had won the peace.

Legacies

The War of 1812 is often called "America's second war of independence," but this overstates what was at stake. Although the issues and ideology echoed those of the Revolution, American independence was never truly at risk. The threat existed mainly in the minds of thin-skinned Republicans who were unable to shed the ideological legacy of the Revolution and interpreted all British actions through this lens.

There is no denying that British encroachments on America rights in this era were both real and serious. But throughout this period Britain's focus was on Europe. Her overriding objective was to defeat Napoleonic France and all else was subordinated to this end. Great Britain's aim, in other words, was not to subvert American independence but to win the war in Europe. Once that objective was achieved, any infringements on American rights would cease.

Besides misreading British intentions, Republicans throughout this turbulent era overrated America's ability to win concessions. "We have considered ourselves of too much importance in the scale of nations," said Virginia Federalist Daniel Sheffey on the eve of the war. "It has led us into great errors. Instead of yielding to circumstances which human power cannot control, we have imagined that our own destiny, and that of other nations, was in our hands, to be regulated as we thought proper." Sheffey's analysis was born out, by not only the failure of the restrictive system but also the futility of the war.

Wartime Leadership

The War of 1812 lasted for two years and eight months—from June 18, 1812, to February 16, 1815. Although by most standards it was not a long war, winning was no easy task, and the nation encountered difficult, if not insuperable, obstacles from the beginning. Many of the nation's military leaders were incompetent, and enlistments in both the army and navy consistently lagged behind need. Relying on militia proved costly and inefficient. Citizen soldiers repeatedly refused to cross into Canada or to hold their positions in the heat of battle. In addition, the Treasury found it difficult to borrow money, and the nation's finances became increasingly chaotic. There was also extensive trade with the enemy, a trade in which Republicans no less than Federalists freely took part. A combination of Republican factionalism, Federalist obstructionism, and general public apathy undermined the entire war effort.

Congress bore some of the responsibility for this state of affairs. Perhaps the endless debate and deep divisions could not be avoided, but there was also an unwillingness to confront the needs of the war. Congress was particularly negligent on financial matters. Hoping for a quick victory and fearing the political consequences of unpopular measures, Congress was slow to adopt internal taxes or to consider a national bank. As a result, public credit collapsed in 1814, and a general suspension of specie payments ensued. If the war had lasted much longer, the Revolutionary War phrase "not worth a Continental" might have been replaced by "not worth a Treasury note."

A strong president might have overcome some of these problems, but James Madison was one of the weakest war leaders in the nation's history. Although Federalists called it "Mr. Madison's War," the contest never bore his stamp. Cautious, shy, and circumspect, Madison was more at home composing legalist diplomatic documents than providing the bold and energetic wartime leadership that was needed. "Mr. Madison is wholly unfit for the storms of war," Henry Clay observed in late 1812. "Nature has cast him in too benevolent a mold." "The amiable temper and delicate sensibility of Mr. Madison," added a fellow Virginia Republican in 1813, "are the real sources of our embarrassments."

In some respects, to be sure, Madison's cautious brand of leadership served the nation well. Unlike other wartime presidents, he was unwilling to use the powers of the government to silence the opposition. Despite pleas from fellow Republicans, he refused to resort to a sedition law to silence critics. Hence, even though Federalists confronted mob violence in 1812, they never had to contend with government repression. The administration's treatment of prisoners of war was also commendably humane, and Madison's restraint in the face of New England disaffection was undoubtedly well judged, too.

In other ways, however, Madison's cautious leadership undermined the war effort. He allowed incompetents like William Eustis and Paul Hamilton to hold key positions, and he tolerated intrigue, backbiting, and insubordination in his cabinet. Madison was also slow to get rid of incompetent generals or to promote those who had proven themselves in battle. Because he lacked influence in Congress, he was unable to secure the passage of vital legislation, and because he lacked a strong following in the country, he was unable to inspire people to open their hearts and purses.

The Cost of the War

Undoubtedly poor leadership in Washington and in the field drove up the cost of the war. The battle casualties were comparatively light: 2,260 Americans were killed and 4,505 were wounded. The number of non-battle deaths will never be known, but a fair estimate would be around 17,000. This figure includes militiamen who contracted fatal camp diseases, seamen who perished in British prisons, and settlers in the West who were victims of Indian raids. The U.S. Army executed 205 men, mainly for repeated desertion, and the U.S. Navy executed a few men, too. In all, the number of American deaths that might be attributed to the war was probably about 20,000. The British, by contrast, lost around 10,000, and the Indians perhaps 7,500.

The financial cost of the war (excluding property damage and lost economic opportunities) was $158 million. This includes $93 million in army and navy expenditures, $16 million for interest on the war loans, and $49 million in veterans' benefits. (The last veteran died in 1905, the last pensioner—the daughter of a veteran—in 1946.) The government also awarded millions of acres of land to some 224,000 men who had served in the war. The national debt, which Republicans had reduced from $83 million in 1801 to $45 million in 1812, soared to $127 million by the end of 1815.

What Did the War Accomplish?

Was the war worth all the blood and treasure expended? Although the conflict ended in a draw on the battlefield, in a larger sense it represented a failure for Republican policy makers. The nation was unable to conquer Canada, and without the leverage that this territory might have afforded, there was no way to force the British to make any concessions on the maritime issues. In fact, these issues were not even mentioned in the peace treaty, which merely provided for restoring all conquered territory and returning to the *status quo ante bellum.*

In other ways, however, the war was fraught with consequences for the future. The United States annexed part of Spanish West Florida in 1813, the only land acquired during the war, although it came at the expense of a neutral power rather than the enemy. The war also broke the power of the Indians in the Old West. The attempts of Tecumseh and the Prophet in the Northwest and William Weatherford and the Red Sticks in the Southwest to halt the tide of American expansion ended in failure. Instead, the Indian wars gave the United States both the excuse and the incentive to accelerate the forced removal of the eastern tribes to lands beyond the Mississippi River.

Never again would Indians seriously threaten the United States, and never again would a Great Power in Europe use Indians in a war against the nation. With the subjugation of the Indians, the westward movement gained momentum, and soon many Americans believed that it was their "manifest destiny" to spread across the continent. The heady nationalism and robust expansionism that characterized American foreign policy throughout the nineteenth century was at least partly a result of the War of 1812.

Even though the war stimulated nationalism, it was also an important benchmark in the history of American sectionalism. In order to retain control over their militia and obstruct the prosecution of a war they considered unwise and unjust, New England Federalists resurrected the states' rights doctrine that Virginia Republicans had used in the late 1790s to resist the alien and sedition laws. This same doctrine would later flourish in the South until the North's victory in the Civil War delivered a body blow to the whole notion of states' rights.

The war also left the United States with an enhanced reputation in Europe. Even though America's performance in the contest was mixed, the Republic emerged intact and had shown that on land and at sea it could hold its own against a Great Power. Europeans no longer assumed that the republican experiment would collapse or that centrifugal forces would tear the Republic apart. "The Americans," said British official Augustus J. Foster, "have had the satisfaction of proving their courage—they have brought us to speak of them with respect."

When the British went back on a war footing after Napoleon returned for his Hundred Days in March 1815, the Royal Navy was careful not to impress any Americans. In fact, Americans were never again subjected to the dubious maritime practices that had caused the war. With Europe generally at peace in the century after Waterloo, the Great Powers had no reason to restrict American trade or to tamper with its seamen. In the meantime, the United States had ample time to grow so that it could meet the Great Powers on an equal footing in the next great conflict—World War I.

The Cultural Legacy

The war gave the nation a set of symbols—"Old Ironsides," the Kentucky rifle, Uncle Sam, the Fort McHenry flag—and sayings—"Don't give up the ship" and "We have met the enemy and they are ours"—that helped shape the American identity. The greatest symbol of all was Andrew Jackson, whose relentless pursuit of the Red Sticks in the Old Southwest and spectacular victory at New Orleans transformed him into an outsized hero who was catapulted into the presidency. Jackson's commitment to frontier democracy, Indian subjugation, slavery, and territorial expansion both reflected and influenced the character of the postwar Republic.

The war also left an enduring legacy of Anglophobia. Hatred of Great Britain, originally kindled by the American Revolution, was further inflamed by the War of 1812. The Indian atrocities in the West and British depredations in the Chesapeake generated considerable bitterness, as did the treatment of prisoners of war. Some

20,000 Americans, mostly seamen serving on privateers, passed through British prisons. Even before the war was over, stories of intolerable conditions and abuse began to filter back to the United States. Once the war was over, this trickle turned into a torrent. "The return of our people from British prisons," said *Niles' Register,* "have filled the newspapers with tales of horror."

Some of the stories came from Melville Island in Halifax, where most Americans captured on the northern frontier were held. "All the prisoners that we have yet seen," said the *Boston Patriot,* "agree that their treatment in the Halifax prisons was brutal and barbarous in the extreme." Other stories came from Dartmoor in southwestern England. By the end of the war, "this accursed place," as one prisoner called it, housed some 5,000 Americans. Trouble at Dartmoor reached a climax on April 6, 1815—almost two months after the war ended—when a dispute over responsibility for transporting the men home delayed repatriation. Anxious to regain their freedom, the prisoners became unruly, and British soldiers fired on them, killing six and wounding sixty others.

Americans did not soon forget the brutality of the war. As early as 1813, the House of Representatives published a study—with extensive documentation—that criticized Great Britain for the Indian atrocities, the Chesapeake depredations, and the mistreatment of prisoners. Other stories kept the embers of hatred alive for decades. Long after the conflict was over, *Niles' Register* published war-related anecdotes and documents that showed the British in a bad light, and nineteenth-century histories continued this tradition by focusing on Britain's misdeeds.

The Military Legacy

The war also stimulated peacetime defense spending. In his message to Congress announcing the end of hostilities, President Madison echoed an old Federalist plea by calling for military preparedness in time of peace. "Experience has taught us," he said, "that a certain degree of preparation for war is not only indispensable to avert disasters in the onset, but affords also the best security for the continuance of peace." Congress agreed. The peacetime army was fixed at 10,000 men in 1815 (three times what it had been in 1802), and the construction of nine ships-of-the-line and twelve heavy frigates was authorized in 1816. Although expenditures for both services were cut back in the wake of the Panic of 1819, the young Republic nevertheless remained committed to the principle of military preparedness. Congress also launched a far-reaching program to fortify the coast, appropriating almost $8,500,000 for this purpose between 1816 and 1829.

The war affected the U.S. military establishment in another way. The U.S. Army, which had entered the war in such a sorry state, emerged as a much improved force with a commitment to professionalism that gave promise of greater success in future wars. Those officers who had outlived their usefulness or failed to live up to expectations—Wilkinson, Hull, Dearborn, Smyth, Hampton, and the like—were cast aside for a new set of officers—Jackson, Brown, Scott, Gaines, and Macomb—who could be counted on to do the job. The U.S. Navy, which had exceeded expectations against the Mistress of the Seas, also boasted a set of officers—Hull, Perry, Macdonough, Porter, Decatur, Bainbridge, and Stewart—who burned their names into the history books. Both services came of age during the war, and both won public esteem that continues to this day.

The Political Legacy

The war also left an enduring political legacy. Four leaders—Jackson, Monroe, Adams, and Harrison—were able to parlay their public service during the war into the presidency. A host of lesser lights also made political capital out of the war. The Battle of the Thames, which became a kind of Bunker Hill in western legend, helped create one president (Harrison), one vice president (Richard M. Johnson), three governors, three lieutenant governors, four U.S. senators, and twenty congressmen, and it served as a stepping stone for countless others who sought lesser offices. In fact, anyone who fought in a battle or even served in the army, navy, or militia during the war had an advantage in any bid for public office.

The war confirmed Republican hegemony and brought the first party system to an end. The Republicans took credit for all the victories and blamed the defeats on the Federalists. The Republicans also charged Federalists with prolonging the war, although the available evidence suggests that leaders on both sides were rendered more amenable to a compromise peace by domestic opposition.

What did the Federalists reap from their opposition to the war? Nothing that was good. Although individual Federalists—such as John Marshall, Daniel Webster, and Josiah Quincy—continued to be active in public life, the party itself never recovered from its opposition nor overcame the taint of treason. The wartime elections suggest that opposition to the conflict was popular during the war but not afterwards. Federalists found it particularly difficult to live down the notoriety of the Hartford Convention.

Federalists protested that they were made the scapegoats for the failure of Republican policies. "The charge that opposition encourages the enemy and injures the cause," said Federalist Rufus King of New York, "has at all times been made as an excuse for the failure and defeat of a weak administration." These protests fell on deaf ears. The decline of the Federalist party—begun in 1800 but arrested by the restrictive system and the war—continued apace after the war was over.

No one seemed to care that the war had vindicated so many Federalist policies, particularly the importance of military and naval preparedness and the need for internal taxes and a national bank, nor did anyone care that Republicans themselves admitted as much by adopting these policies during or after the war. It mattered not that Federalists had predicted the futility of the conflict and that the Treaty of Ghent had proven them right. What mattered was that the nation had emerged from the war without surrendering any rights or territory and with just enough triumphs—both on land and at sea—to give the appearance of victory.

The Myth of American Victory

Although fought after Great Britain had signed and ratified the treaty, the Battle of New Orleans played a particularly important role in forging the myth of American victory. The news of Jackson's great victory arrived in the nation's capital on February 4, 1815. The news of peace followed ten days later. The sequence was similar elsewhere and helped create the impression that Jackson's victory had influenced the peace terms. Even before those terms were known, Republicans were touting New Orleans as a decisive turning point in the war. "The terms of the treaty are yet unknown to us," said Congressman Charles J. Ingersoll in early 1815. "But the victory at Orleans has rendered them glorious and honorable, be they what they may."

In the years that followed, memories faded, and the link between the victory at New Orleans and honorable peace terms became ever more pronounced. Republicans boasted of how they had defeated "the heroes of Wellington," "Wellington's invincibles," and "the conquerors of the conquerors of Europe." The myth of American victory continued to grow so that by 1816 *Niles' Register* could unabashedly claim that "we did virtually dictate the Treaty of Ghent."

As the years slipped by, most people forgot the causes of the war. They forgot the defeats on land and sea and lost sight of how close the nation had come to military defeat and financial collapse. According to the emerging myth, the United States had won the war as well as the peace. Thus, the War of 1812 passed into history not as a futile and costly struggle in which America had barely escaped defeat and disunion, but as a glorious triumph in which the nation had single-handedly defeated the conqueror of Napoleon and the Mistress of the Seas.

Chronology

The following chronology presents the dates for events mentioned in the text. The more important events are in **bold** type. Numbers in parentheses indicate number of guns on an armed ship.

1789–1801	Federalists in power
1789	
April 30:	George Washington inaugurated as president of U.S. in New York City
July 14:	Mob storms Bastille in Paris (French Revolution begins)
1789–1794	U.S. adopts Alexander Hamilton's financial program
1792	
April 20:	France declares war on Austria (French Revolutionary Wars begin)
1793	
February 1:	France declares war on Great Britain
1794	
November 19:	U.S. and Great Britain sign Jay Treaty in London
1797	
March 4:	John Adams inaugurated as president of U.S. in Philadelphia
1798–1801	U.S. and France wage Quasi-War
1801–1815	Republicans in power
1801	
March 4:	Thomas Jefferson inaugurated as president of U.S. in Washington, D.C.

October 1:	Great Britain and France sign preliminary Treaty of Amiens (French Revolutionary Wars end)
1801–1802	U.S. adopts retrenchment policy
1803	
May 17:	Great Britain issues letters of marque and reprisal against France (Napoleonic Wars begin)
October 1:	Commercial clauses in Jay Treaty expire
1805	
October 21:	Battle of Trafalgar off coast of Spain in Atlantic
December 2:	Battle of Austerlitz (Czech Republic)
1806	
April 18:	U.S. adopts (but suspends) partial non-importation law against Great Britain
December 31:	U.S. and Great Britain sign Monroe–Pinkney Treaty in London
1806–1807	France issues Continental Decrees
1807	
March 3:	U.S. rejects Monroe–Pinkney Treaty
June 22:	*Chesapeake* affair
December 14:	U.S. activates partial non-importation law of 1806
December 22:	U.S. adopts embargo prohibiting U.S. ships and goods from leaving port
1807–1809	Great Britain issues Orders-in-Council
1809	
March 1:	U.S. adopts non-intercourse law against Great Britain and France
March 4:	James Madison inaugurated as president of U.S. in Washington, D.C.
September 30:	U.S. and Delawares, Miamis, Potawatomis, and Eel River Miamis sign Treaty of Fort Wayne (Ind.)
1811	
March 2:	U.S. adopts non-importation law against Great Britain
May 16:	*Little Belt* affair
November 4:	War Congress convenes in Washington, D.C.
November 5:	President Madison recommends war preparations
November 7:	Battle of Tippecanoe (Ind.)
November 8:	U.S. burns Prophetstown (Ind.)

November 12:	U.S. and Great Britain settle *Chesapeake* affair in Washington, D.C.
December 24–April 10:	U.S. adopts war preparations
1812	
March 9:	President Madison publicizes John Henry spy mission
May 22:	Dispatches from USS *Hornet* (20) reach Washington, D.C.
May 27:	Great Britain offers to share license trade with U.S.
June 1:	President Madison sends war message to U.S. Congress
June 4:	U.S. House of Representatives adopts war bill
June 16:	Great Britain announces offer to suspend Orders-in-Council
June 17:	U.S. Senate adopts war bill
June 18:	**President Madison signs war bill into law (War of 1812 begins)**
June 18–26:	U.S. sends out peace feelers
June 22–August 4:	Baltimore Riots
June 23:	France invades Russia
June 23:	**Great Britain revokes Orders-in-Council**
June 23:	USS *President* (54) clashes with HMS *Belvidera* (42) in North Atlantic
July 1:	U.S. doubles customs duties
July 2:	Great Britain captures *Cuyahoga* in Detroit River
July 6:	U.S. adopts first enemy trade law
July 12:	U.S. invades Canada across Detroit River
July 12:	Brig. Gen. William Hull issues proclamation at Sandwich (Ont.) promising to liberate Canada
July 16:	British squadron captures USS *Nautilus* (14) in North Atlantic
July 16–19:	USS *Constitution* (55) outruns British squadron in North Atlantic
July 17:	**Great Britain captures Fort Mackinac (Mich.)**
July 30:	News of war reaches London
August 7:	U.S. withdraws from Canada across Detroit River
August 13:	News of repeal of Orders-in-Council reaches Washington, D.C.
August 13:	USS *Essex* (46) captures HMS *Alert* (18?) in North Atlantic

August 15:	Fort Dearborn (Ill.) Massacre
August 16:	**Great Britain captures Detroit**
August 19:	USS *Constitution* (55) defeats HMS *Guerrière* (49) in North Atlantic
September–November:	**State elections ensure President Madison's re-election**
October–November:	Great Britain establishes a blockade from Charleston (S.C.) to St. Marys (Ga.)
October 8–9:	U.S. destroys Provincial Marine Brig *Detroit* (6) and captures Provincial Marine Brig *Caledonia* (3) on Niagara River
October 13:	**Battle of Queenston Heights (Ont.)**; Maj. Gen. Isaac Brock killed
October 13:	**Great Britain authorizes general reprisals against U.S.**
October 18:	USS *Wasp* (18) defeats HMS *Frolic* (22) in North Atlantic
October 18:	HMS *Poictiers* (80) captures USS *Wasp* (18) in North Atlantic
October 19–December 14:	France retreats from Russia
October 25:	USS *United States* (56) captures HMS *Macedonian* (49) in North Atlantic
November 19:	U.S. invades Lower Canada (Que.)
November 20:	Battle of Lacolle Mill (Que.)
November 22:	HMS *Southampton* (41) captures USS *Vixen* (14) in North Atlantic
November 23:	U.S. withdraws from Lower Canada (Que.)
November 28:	U.S. attacks Fort Erie (Ont.)
December 17–18:	Battle of Mississinewa (Ind.)
December 23:	Bennington (Vt.) *News-Letter* publishes first reference to "Uncle Sam"
December 29:	USS *Constitution* (54) defeats HMS *Java* (49) off coast of Brazil in Atlantic; Capt. Henry Lambert killed

1813

January 22:	**Battle of Frenchtown (Mich.)**
January 23:	**River Raisin (Mich.) Massacre**
February 6:	**Great Britain proclaims blockade of Delaware and Chesapeake bays**
February 24:	USS *Hornet* (20) defeats HMS *Peacock* (20) off coast of Guiana in Atlantic
March 8:	Russia offers to mediate end to War of 1812

March 11:	U.S. accepts Russia's mediation offer
March 19:	Capt. James Yeo appointed commander of British warships on Great Lakes
April 15:	U.S. occupies West Florida
April 27:	**U.S. captures York (Ont.)**
April 29:	Great Britain raids Frenchtown (Md.)
April 29:	Battle of Fort Defiance (Md.)
May:	U.S. circuit court renders *Julia* decision in Boston
May 1–9:	**First Siege of Fort Meigs (Ohio)**
May 3:	Great Britain burns Havre de Grace (Md.)
May 3:	Great Britain destroys Principio Ironworks (Md.)
May 5:	Great Britain routs U.S. relief force at Fort Meigs
May 5:	Massacre of U.S. POWs near Fort Meigs
May 6:	Great Britain burns Fredericktown and Georgetown (Md.)
May 26:	**Great Britain proclaims blockade of major ports in middle and southern states**
May 27:	**U.S. captures Fort George (Ont.)**
May 28:	Great Britain evacuates all posts along Niagara River
May 29:	**Battle of Sackets Harbor (N.Y.)**
June 1:	HMS *Shannon* (52) defeats USS *Chesapeake* (50) off coast of Massachusetts in Atlantic; Capt. James Lawrence killed
June 5–6:	**Battle of Stoney Creek (Ont.)**
June 22:	Battle of Craney Island (Va.)
June 22–23:	Laura Secord's trek (Ont.)
June 24:	**Battle of Beaver Dams (Ont.)**
June 25:	Great Britain attacks Hampton (Va.)
July 5:	Great Britain rejects Russia's mediation offer
July 21–28:	**Second siege of Fort Meigs (Ohio)**
July 24–August 2:	U.S. adopts internal taxes
July 27:	Battle of Burnt Corn (Ala.)
August 1–2:	**Battle of Fort Stephenson (Ohio)**
August 2:	U.S. adopts law barring use of enemy licenses
August 4?:	Great Britain occupies Kent Island (Md.)
August 8:	USS *Hamilton* (9) and USS *Scourge* (10) capsize and sink in Lake Ontario

August 10:	Great Britain raids St. Michaels (Md.)
August 13:	Battle of Queenstown (Md.)
August 14:	HMS *Pelican* (21) defeats USS *Argus* (20) off coast of Ireland in Atlantic
August 26:	Great Britain raids St. Michaels (Md.)
August 30:	**Fort Mims Massacre (Ala.)**
September 5:	USS *Enterprise* (16) defeats HMS *Boxer* (14) off coast of Maine in Atlantic; Commander Samuel Blyth and Lieutenant William Burrows killed
September 10:	**Battle of Lake Erie**
September 18:	Great Britain evacuates Fort Detroit
September 27:	U.S. occupies Fort Detroit and Fort Amherstburg (Ont.)
September 28:	"Burlington Races" on Lake Ontario
October 5:	**Battle of the Thames/Moraviantown (Ont.)**; Tecumseh killed
October 16–19:	Battle of Leipzig (Germany)
October 26:	**Battle of Châteauguay (Que.)**
November 3:	Battle of Tallushatchee (Ala.)
November 4:	Great Britain offers U.S. direct peace negotiations
November 9:	Battle of Talladega (Ala.)
November 11:	**Battle of Crysler's Farm (Ont.)**
November 16:	**Great Britain proclaims blockade of Long Island Sound and remaining ports in middle and southern states**
December 10:	U.S. evacuates Fort George and burns Newark (Ont.)
December 12:	Great Britain occupies Fort George (Ont.)
December 17:	U.S. adopts embargo barring all U.S. ships and goods from leaving port
December 19:	**Great Britain captures Fort Niagara (N.Y.)**
December 19–21:	Great Britain burns Lewiston, Youngstown, and Manchester (N.Y.)
December 30:	Great Britain burns Buffalo and Black Rock (N.Y.)
1814	
January 22:	Battle of Emuckfau Creek (Ala.)
January 24:	Battle of Enotachopco Creek (Ala.)
March 26:	U.S. military court in Albany finds Brig. Gen. William Hull guilty of cowardice and neglect of duty
March 27–28:	**Battle of Horseshoe Bend (Ala.)**

March 28:	HMS *Phoebe* (46 or 53) and HMS *Cherub* (26) defeat USS *Essex* (46) off coast of Chile in Pacific
March 31:	European allies enter Paris
April 2:	Great Britain issues proclamation urging slaves in Chesapeake to run away
April 7–8:	Great Britain raids Pettipaug Point (Conn.)
April 11:	Napoleon abdicates throne unconditionally
April 14:	U.S. repeals embargo and non-importation law
April 25:	**Great Britain proclaims blockade of New England**
April 28:	Napoleon exiled to Elba in Mediterranean
April 29:	USS *Peacock* (22) defeats HMS *Epervier* (18) in Caribbean
May 6:	Great Britain captures Oswego (N.Y.)
May 14–15:	U.S. raids Dover (Ont.)
May 30:	Battle of Sandy Creek (N.Y.)
May 30:	European allies and France sign First Treaty of Paris (Napoleonic Wars suspended)
June 2:	U.S. captures Prairie du Chien (Wis.)
June 9–10:	Militiamen carry great rope from Sandy Creek to Sackets Harbor (N.Y.)
June 27:	**U.S. drops impressment demand**
June 28:	USS *Wasp* (22) defeats HMS *Reindeer* (19) in North Atlantic
July 3:	U.S. captures Fort Erie (Ont.)
July 5:	**Battle of Chippawa (Ont.)**
July 11:	Great Britain captures Eastport (Maine)
July 20:	Great Britain recaptures Prairie du Chien (Wis.)
July 22:	U.S. and Miamis, Potawatomis, Ottawas, Shawnees, Kickapoos sign peace treaty at Greenville (Ohio)
July 25:	**Battle of Lundy's Lane (Ont.)**
August:	U.S. public credit collapses
August:	U.S. banks suspend specie payments
August 4:	U.S. attacks Fort Mackinac (Mich.)
August 8:	**Peace negotiations begin at Ghent (Belgium)**
August 9:	U.S. and Creeks sign peace treaty at Fort Jackson (Ala.)
August 9–11:	Battle of Stonington (Conn.)
August 14:	Great Britain occupies Pensacola (Fla.)
August 15:	**Battle of Fort Erie (Ont.)**

August 19–20:	Great Britain lands at Benedict (Md.) en route to Washington
August 22:	U.S. blows up its Chesapeake flotilla at Pig Point (Md.)
August 24:	**Battle of Bladensburg (Md.)**
August 24:	U.S. burns Washington Naval Yard, USS *Columbia* (rated 44), and USS *Argus* (rated 18)
August 24–25:	**Great Britain occupies Washington, D.C.**
August 27:	Capt. Thomas Boyle of U.S. privateer *Chasseur* (16) proclaims mock blockade of Great Britain and Ireland
August 28:	Nantucket (Mass.) declares neutrality
August 29:	Great Britain captures Alexandria (Va.)
August 31:	Battle of Caulk's Field (Md.); Capt. Peter Parker killed
August 31:	Great Britain invades New York
September 1:	USS *Wasp* (22) defeats HMS *Avon* (20) in North Atlantic
September 1–11:	**Great Britain occupies 100 miles of U.S. coast from Eastport to Castine (Maine)**
September 3:	Great Britain captures USS *Tigress* (1) on Lake Huron
September 6:	Great Britain captures USS *Scorpion* (2) on Lake Huron
September 11:	Battle of Plattsburgh (N.Y.)
September 11:	**Battle of Lake Champlain**; Capt. George Downie killed
September 12:	**Battle of North Point**; Maj. Gen. Robert Ross killed
September 13–14:	**Great Britain bombards Fort McHenry (Md.)**
September 14:	Great Britain withdraws from Baltimore
September 14:	Francis Scott Key writes "The Star-Spangled Banner"
September 15–June 9:	Congress of Vienna meets (Austria)
September 17:	**U.S. sortie from Fort Erie**
September 26–27:	British squadron defeats U.S. privateer *General Armstrong* (9) in Azores
October 11:	U.S. privateer *Prince-de-Neufchatel* (17) defeats flotilla of boats from HMS *Endymion* (47) near Nantucket in Atlantic
October 19:	Battle of Cook's Mills (Ont.)
October 22–November 17:	Brig. Gen. Duncan McArthur's Raid (Ont.)
November 5:	U.S. evacuates Fort Erie (Ont.)
November 6:	Battle of Malcolm's Mills (Ont.)
December 14:	**Battle of Lake Borgne (La.)**

December 15–January 5:	Hartford Convention meets
December 15–February 27:	U.S. adopts internal taxes
December 16:	Maj. Gen. Andrew Jackson proclaims martial law in New Orleans
December 23:	Battle of Villeré's Plantation (La.)
December 24:	**U.S. and Great Britain sign Treaty of Ghent**
December 27:	British artillery destroys USS *Carolina* (13)
December 27:	**Great Britain ratifies Treaty of Ghent**
December 28:	British Reconnaissance in Force at New Orleans
December 28:	U.S. Congress rejects conscription

1815

January 1:	Battle of Rodriquez Canal/Artillery Duel at New Orleans
January 2:	HMS *Favourite* (26?) departs from Britain with Treaty of Ghent
January 8:	**Battle of New Orleans**; Maj. Gen. Edward Pakenham and Maj. Gen. Samuel Gibbs killed
January 9–18:	Great Britain Bombards Fort St. Philip (La.)
January 10–11:	Great Britain occupies Cumberland Island (Ga.)
January 13:	Great Britain attacks Point Peter on Cumberland Island
January 15:	British squadron captures USS *President* (53)
January 28:	British military court in Montreal finds Maj. Gen. Henry Procter guilty of mismanaging Thames campaign
February 4:	U.S. adopts second enemy trade law
February 11:	HMS *Favourite* (26?) reaches New York City with Treaty of Ghent
February 8–11:	Siege of Fort Bowyer (Ala.)
February 14:	Treaty of Ghent reaches Washington, D.C.
February 16:	U.S. Senate unanimously approves Treaty of Ghent
February 16:	**President Madison ratifies Treaty of Ghent (War of 1812 officially ends)**
February 17:	U.S. Congress rejects national bank
February 17:	**U.S. and Great Britain exchange ratifications of Treaty of Ghent (treaty becomes binding)**
February 20:	USS *Constitution* (52) defeats HMS *Cyane* (33) and HMS *Levant* (21) off coast of North Africa in Atlantic
February 21:	U.S. executes 6 militiamen in Mobile (Ala.)

February 24:	U.S. ambushes British force in St. Marys River (Ga.)
February 26:	U.S. privateer *Chasseur* (14) defeats HMS *St. Lawrence* (15) off coast of Cuba in Caribbean
March 13:	Official news of peace reaches New Orleans
March 13:	Maj. Gen. Andrew Jackson lifts martial law in New Orleans
March 23:	USS *Hornet* (20) defeats HMS *Penguin* (19) near Tristan da Cunha in Atlantic
March 28:	News of peace reaches London
March 31:	Maj. Gen. Andrew Jackson convicted of contempt and fined $1,000 (La.)
April 6:	Dartmoor Massacre (Great Britain)
1815–16	U.S. and western Indian tribes sign peace treaties

Suggestions for Further Reading

The best starting point for any reading on the War of 1812 is a bibliography. The most useful are John C. Fredriksen, *Free Trade and Sailors' Rights: A Bibliography of the War of 1812* (1985), and Dwight L. Smith, *The War of 1812: An Annotated Bibliography* (1985). For an assessment of best books on the war and its causes, see my article, "The Top 25 Books on the War of 1812," *War of 1812 Magazine* 2 (September, 2007) at http://www.napoleon-series.org/military/Warof1812/2007/Issue7/c_top25books.html.

There are several good military histories of the war. The best of the older studies are John K. Mahon's *War of 1812* (1972) and Reginald Horsman's *The War of 1812* (1969). Of the recent popular studies, the most serviceable is Walter R. Borneman, *1812: The War That Forged a Nation* (2004). For a thorough account of the land war, see Robert S. Quimby, *The U.S. Army in the War of 1812: An Operational and Command Study*, 2 vols. (1997). In a category by itself is the classic study by Benson J. Lossing, *The Pictorial Field-Book of the War of 1812* (1868), which is available in several modern editions. Lossing traveled 10,000 miles in the 1850s and 1860s, visiting battle sites and interviewing survivors. His work is a compendium of fascinating detail that includes songs, poems, battle maps, and illustrations.

For the British/Canadian side of the story, the best account is J. Mackay Hitsman, *The Incredible War of 1812: A Military History*, updated by Donald E. Graves (1999). Also useful is George F. G. Stanley, *The War of 1812: Land Operations* (1983), which has particularly good maps. For the role of Indians in the war, see Robert S. Allen, *His Majesty's Indian Allies: British Indian Policy in the Defence of Canada, 1774–1815* (1993); Carl Benn, *The Iroquois in the War of 1812* (1999); and R. David Edmunds, *The Shawnee Prophet* (1983), and *Tecumseh and the Quest for Indian Leadership*, 2nd, ed. (2007).

There are several fine regional studies. For the war in the Old Northwest, see Sandy Antal, *A Wampum Denied: Procter's War of 1812*, 2nd ed. (2011). The best accounts of the fighting on the Niagara frontier are the battle studies of Donald E. Graves, especially *Where Right and Glory Lead! The Battle of Lundy's Lane, 1814*, rev. ed. (1997). For the war in the Lake Champlain-Richelieu River corridor, see Allan S. Everest, *The War of 1812 in the Champlain Valley* (1981). For a fine attempt to apply the "new" history (particularly the notions of clashing cultures, contested borders, and uncertain loyalties) to the Canadian-American frontier, see Alan Taylor, *The Civil War of 1812: American Citizens, British Subjects, Irish Rebels, and Indian Allies* (2010).

For the war in the Chesapeake, Walter Lord, *The Dawn's Early Light* (1972), is still useful, but see also Christopher T. George, *Terror on the Chesapeake: The War of 1812 on the Bay* (2000). For the war in the Southwest and on the Gulf Coast, the best works are Frank L. Owsley, Jr., *Struggle for the Gulf Borderlands: The Creek War and the Battle of New Orleans, 1812–1815* (Gainesville, 1981), and Robin Reilly, *The British at the Gates: The New Orleans Campaign in the War of 1812*, rev. ed. (Toronto, 2002).

The best accounts of the war at sea are still Theodore Roosevelt, *The Naval History of the War of 1812*, 7th. ed., 2 vols. (1900), which is available in several modern editions and judiciously treats the battles; and Alfred T. Mahan, *Sea Power and its Relations to the War of 1812*, 2 vols. (1905), which deals with the larger issues of naval strategy. For a good recent study that stresses personalities and the management of the war from the shore, see Stephen Budiansky, *Perilous Fight: America's Intrepid War with Britain on the High Seas, 1812–1815* (2010). For the impact of the British blockade, see Brian Arthur, *How Britain Won the War of 1812: The Royal Navy's Blockades of the United States, 1812–1815* (2011).

The best study of privateering is still Edgar S. Maclay, *A History of American Privateers* (1899). Jerome R. Garitee, *The Republic's Private Navy: The American Privateering Business as Practiced by Baltimore during the War of 1812* (1977), is a good study of the in-port side of privateering.

For the domestic history of the war, readers should consult my longer work, *The War of 1812: A Forgotten Conflict*, bicentennial ed. (2012), which examines the political, economic, and financial history of the contest; and J. C. A. Stagg's *Mr. Madison's War: Politics, Diplomacy, and Warfare in the Early American Republic, 1783–1830* (1983), which traces the inner history of the Republican party and explores the impact of politics on the prosecution of the war. For a balanced account of President Madison's wartime leadership, see Robert A. Rutland, *The Presidency of James Madison* (1990).

Index

Adams, John Quincy, 3, 105–6, 110–11, 120
Adams, USS, 32, 83
Adams, William, 106
Afghanistan War, 1
Albany Congress, 100
Alert, HMS, 37
Alexandria (Va.), 55, 75, 77
alien laws, 6, 118
Amelia Island (Florida), 94
American Revolution, 1, 3, 6, 23, 70, 116; echoed
    by War of 1812, 3, 18, 115; generates anglopho-
    bia, 4, 6, 118
Amiens, Peace of, 7
Anacostia River, 72
Anglo-French wars, 5. *See also* Napoleonic Wars
Anglophobia: generated by American Revolu-
    tion, 4, 6, 118; stimulated by *Chesapeake* af-
    fair, 9; stimulated by War of 1812, 3, 18, 115
Argus, USS (rated 18 guns), 74
Argus, USS (20 guns), 57
Armistead, George, 77
Armstrong, John, 40–41, 61, 66, 72, 74, 88
Army, British, 23, 40, 60
Army, U.S.: bounties for, 33, 40, 91; condition
    of, 21, 32, 40, 60–61, 64; and conscription,
    90; daily ration of, 22; desertion from, 21, 83,
    117; executions in, 117; leadership in 3, 7, 21,
    40, 61; and legacy of war, 119–20; payment of,
    21–22; size of, 6–7, 12, 40, 61, 90; supply of,
    22–23, 28; weapons of, 22–23
arsenals, U.S., 22, 74
artillery, U.S., 22
Artillery Duel (La.), 81

Atlantic coast, 94. *See also* blockade, naval: of
    British
Avon, HMS, 84
Azores, 85

Bainbridge, William, 35–36, 120
Baker, Anthony, 111–12
Baltimore, 54–55; British attack on, 3, 72, 75–77,
    85, 109; as privateering base, 75, 85; prowar
    riots in, 98
banks, 92, 100. *See also* national bank
Baratarian pirates, 79, 94
Barclay, Robert H, 43–44
Barney, Joshua, 37, 71, 73–74
Bass Islands (Ohio), 43
Bayard, James A., 105–6
Baynes, Edward, 49–50
Beasley, Daniel, 51
Beaver Dams (Ont.), Battle of, 48
Beckwith, Thomas Sidney, 55
belligerent rights, 6
Benedict (Md.), 72
black people, 78–79. *See also* slaves
Black Rock (N.Y.), 41, 43, 49
Bladensburg (Md.), Battle of, 72–73
"Bladensburg races," 73
blockade, naval: of British, 8, 15–16, 33, 54–55,
    68–69, 83, 103, 110; of U.S. privateer *Chas-
    seur,* 85
Block Island (R.I.), 70
Bloomfield, Joseph, 31
Boerstler, Charles, 48
Bonaparte. *See* Napoleon

Boston, 55, 112

Boundary convention (1803), 111

Boxer, HMS, 56–57

Boyd, John P., 50

Boyle, Thomas, 85

British Isles: and British privateering, 37; and Continental Decrees, 9; and prisoners of war, 97; and U.S. privateering, 58–59, 84

British Reconnaissance in Force (La.), 80

Brock, Isaac, 27, 30, 41

Broke, Philip, 57–58

Brooke, Arthur, 76

Brown, Jacob, 40, 86; and Battle of Sackets Harbor, 49–50; impact of war on career of, 1, 3, 120; and Niagara campaign of 1814, 62–65

Buffalo (N.Y.), 20, 41, 49

Bunker Hill (Mass.), Battle of, 120

Burgoyne, John, 66

Burlington Heights (Ont.), 46, 48

Burnt Corn (Ala.), Battle of, 51–52

Byron, Lord, 75

cabinet, U.S.: and maritime war, 16; troubles in, 40, 74, 87–88, 116

Caledonia, Prov. Marine, 42

Calhoun, John C., 3, 16, 93

Campbell, John B., 61

Canada: boundary with U.S., 70, 111; and British coastal raids on U.S., 55, 71, 78; and causes of war, 2, 19; and peace negotiations, 70, 104–5, 107; and prewar Indian raids, 11; U.S. attempts to conquer, 3, 12, 16–20, 23–32, 38, 51, 61–65, 87, 103, 112, 117; U.S. trade with, 94–95

Canadian Volunteers, 62

Canoe Fight, 52

Cape Cod (Mass.), 69, 94

Capitol, U.S., 5, 74

Carden, John S, 36–37

Carolina, USS, 80

Carroll, Henry, 111–12

Castine (Maine), 70

Castlereagh, Lord, 15, 104–6

casualties, 117

Caulk's Field (Md.), Battle of, 75

cease-fire. *See* Prevost, George: and armistice of 1812

Charleston (So. Car.), 54–55

Chasseur, U.S. privateer, 85

Châteauguay (Que.), Battle of, 50

Chauncey, Isaac, 41, 46; and Battle of Fort George, 47; and Battle of Sackets Harbor, 49; and Battle of York, 46–47; and "Burlington

Races," 46; orders Elliott to Lake Erie, 41; orders Perry to Lake Erie, 42–43

Cherub, HMS, 83

Chesapeake, USS, 32, 57–58

Chesapeake affair, 8–10, 14

Chesapeake Bay, 1, 87; blockaded by British, 54; and enemy trade, 94; invaded by British, 55–56, 70–77, 92, 103; and legacy of war, 118–19

Cheves, Langdon, 93

Chippawa (Ont.), Battle of, 62, 103

Choctaw Indians, 80

Christmas Eve, Peace of, 2, 107–13, 120

Chubb, HMS, 66

Civil War, U.S., 1, 3, 92, 118

Claiborne, William, 79

Clark, Allen, 65

Clay, Henry: on conquest of Canada, 19–20; impact of war on career of, 3; leading War Hawk, 11–12; on Madison's leadership, 116; and peace negotiations, 106–11; supports wartime restrictive system, 93

Clinton, De Witt, 88–90

Clintonians, 88

Cochrane, Alexander, 72, 75–76, 79

Cockburn, George, 55–56, 72–74, 77

Coffee, John, 79

Columbia, USS, 74

commerce. *See* trade

commercial restrictions. *See* restrictive system

commissary department, 22

Confiance, HMS, 66–67

Congress, U.S.: and declaration of war, 16–17; factionalism in, 11–12, 88, 116; political complexion of, 11, 90; and war preparations, 12–13

Congress, USS, 32

Congreve rockets, 73, 77

Connecticut, 69, 99–102

conscription, 90, 101

Constellation, USS, 32, 55

Constitution, USS, 4, 32–36, 84, 118

constitutional amendments, 90

Constitutional Convention, Philadelphia, 101

Continental Congress, First, 101

Continental Decrees, 9, 15

contraband, 8

Craney Island (Va.), Battle of, 55–56

credit, public, U.S., 92, 116

Creek War, 51–54

Croghan, George, 41

Cryslers's Farm (Ont.), Battle of, 50–51

Cumberland Head (N.Y.), 67

Cumberland Island (Ga.), 77–78

customs revenue, U.S. *See* taxes
Cuyahoga, U.S. ship, 26
Cyane, HMS, 84

Dacres, James R., 34–35
Dale, Sam, 52
Dartmoor prison (Eng.), 96, 119
Dashkov, Andrei, 105
Dearborn, Henry, 26, 31, 46–48, 104, 120
Decatur, Stephen, 36–37, 83, 120
declaration of war, 15–18, 103–4
"Defence of Fort McHenry, The," 77
Delaware Bay, 54
Demologos, USS, 84
Detroit, HMS, 43
Detroit (Mich.), 1, 20, 87; as base for U.S. raids,
  61; captured by British, 26–29, 31, 41–42; and
  peace negotiations, 109; recaptured by U.S.,
  44, 68
Detroit, Prov. Marine, 42
Dobbins, Daniel, 41
"Don't give up the ship," 4, 57–58, 60, 118
"Don't give up the soil," 60
Downie, George, 66–67
Drummond, Gordon, 49, 62–65
Drummond, William, 64

Eagle, USS, 66–67
Eastport (Maine), 70
economy, U.S., 6, 9, 54–55, 69, 95
Eisenhower, Dwight, 1
elections, 6, 88–92, 120
Elkton (Md.), 55
Elliott, Jesse, 41–42
Elliott, Matthew, 42
embargo: of 1807, 9, 97; of 1812, 13–14, 93; of
  1813, 95; and Hartford Convention, 102
Emuckfau (Ala.), Battle of, 52
Endymion, HMS, 83, 85
enemy trade act, 93–96
English Channel, 85
Enotachopco Creek (Ala.), Battle of, 32
Enterprise, USS, 56–57
Epervier, HMS, 84
Era of Good Feelings, 3–4
Erie (Penn.), 41, 43
Essex (Conn.), 69
Essex, USS, 32, 37, 83
Eustis, William, 20–21, 40, 116
exports, U.S. *See* trade

factionalism. *See* Republican party
Favourite, HMS, 111–12

Federalist party: ascendancy of, 5–6; broad
  objectives of, 5; and declaration of war, 13–14,
  16–18; and elections, 6, 89–90; impact of war
  on, 4; and inner war, 87–88; opposes war,
  2, 97–102; policies of vindicated, 4, 120–21;
  response of to peace, 112–13; and war prepa-
  rations, 12
finance, wartime, 2–3, 91–93,117. *See also* loans;
  taxes; Treasury notes
Finch, HMS, 66
Fischer, Victor, 63
Fishing, U.S., 69, 107, 110
FitzGibbon, James, 48
Florida (Spanish), 51, 54, 78–79, 94, 117
Fort Dearborn (Ill.) Massacre, 27–29
Fort Detroit (Mich.), 27, 44. *See also* Detroit
  (Mich.)
Fort Erie (Ont.), 30, 42, 47–48, 62–64, 103, 109
Fort George (Ont.), 30, 47–49
fortifications, coastal, 6, 12, 91, 99, 119
Fort Jackson (Ala.), Treaty of, 54
Fort Mackinac (Mich.), 61. *See also* Mackinac
Fort McHenry (Md.), 1, 4, 76–77, 103
Fort Meigs (Ont.), 42
Fort Mims (Ala.) Massacre, 51–52
Fort Niagara (N.Y.), 47, 49, 67, 109
Fort Stephenson (Ohio), 42
Fort Tompkins (N.Y.), 49
Fort Washington (Va.), 75
Foster, Augustus J., 14, 104, 118
France, 6, 9, 16–17, 39–40, 60, 98, 107
Fredericktown (Md.), 55
"Free Trade and Sailors' Rights," 2, 17, 57–58,
  60
French Revolution, 5
French Revolutionary Wars, 5
Frenchtown (Md.), 55
Frenchtown (Mich.), Battle of, 28–29, 31, 51
Frolic, HMS, 37
Frolic, USS, 84
Fulton (N.Y.), 65
Fulton, Robert, 84
Fulton the First, USS, 84

Gaillard, John, 17
Gaines, Edmund, 22, 63–64, 120
Gallatin, Albert, 91–92, 102, 105–6
Gambier, Lord, 106
General Armstrong, U.S. privateer, 85
General Pike, USS, 46
Georgetown (Md.), 55
Georgia, 51–52
Ghent (Belgium), 103, 107

Ghent, Treaty of, 2, 107–13, 120
Gothenburg (Sweden), 107
Goulburn, Henry, 106
Grand Terre Island (La.), 94
Granger, Gideon, 88
Grant, Ulysses S., 1
Great Britain: and coming of war, 2, 8–11, 14–15, 104; and peace negotiations, 104–11
Great Lakes, 23, 41, 44, 107. *See also* Lake Erie; Lake Ontario
Greenville, Treaty of (1795), 107–8
Gregg, Andrew, 17
Grundy, Felix, 98
Guerrière, HMS, 34–35
Gulf Coast, U.S., 1, 21, 77–82, 87, 94, 109
gunboats, 7, 33, 44, 65–66, 71, 80

Halifax (Nova Scotia), 14, 20, 33–34, 37, 56–57, 84; and peace negotiations, 70, 107, 109; and prisoners of war, 96, 119
Hamilton, Alexander, 5–6
Hamilton (Ont.), 46. *See also* Burlington Heights
Hamilton, Paul, 32, 40, 116
Hamilton, USS, 46
Hampton (Va.), 56
Hampton, Wade, 50, 120
Hanson, Alexander, 98
Harpers Ferry (Va.), 22–23
Harpy, U.S. privateer, 85
Harrison, William Henry, 1, 3, 40, 44, 120; assumes command in Old Northwest, 28; and Battle of Thames, 44–45, 54; and Battle of Tippecanoe, 10–11; and defense of Fort Meigs, 42
Hartford (Conn.), 99
Hartford Convention, 100–102, 120
Havre de Grace (Md.), 55
Heald, Nathan, 27–28
Henry, John, 13, 16
Hornet, USS, 13, 15, 37, 57
Hornet, USS (built during war), 84
Horseshoe Bend (Ala.), Battle of, 52–54, 103
House, U.S. *See* Congress, U.S.
Hull, Isaac, 34–35, 120
Hull, William, 20, 26–27, 31, 120
Humphreys, Joshua, 32

ideology, as a cause of war, 3, 15, 17
imports, U.S. *See* trade
impressment, 8, 33, 188; as a cause of war, 2, 8, 11; and *Chesapeake* affair, 8–9; and Monroe-

Pinkney Treaty, 8; and peace negotiations, 104–7, 110, 117
Independence, USS, 84
independent companies of foreigners, 56
Indians: atrocities of, 28; British influence over, 2, 10–11; casualties of, 117; and causes of war, 2, 16–17; impact of war on, 4, 117–18; and peace, 46, 107–8, 110–11. *See also individual tribes*
Ingersoll, Charles J., 121
insurance rates, 13, 55, 84, 91
"Invisibles," Senate, 88
Iraq War, 1
Irishmen, 97
Irish Sea, 84
"Ironsides." See *Constitution*

Jackson, Andrew, 40; and Creek War, 52–54; dictatorial methods of, 82–83; and Gulf Coast campaign, 1, 3, 78–82, 86, 102–3, 121; impact of war on career of, 1, 3, 118, 120
Jamaica, 34, 79
Java, HMS, 35–36
Jay Treaty, 6, 8, 107, 111
Jefferson, Thomas, 5, 8, 20, 38, 60, 93, 98
Johnson, John (Richard's brother), 45
Johnson, Richard M., 3, 44–45, 120
Jones, Gordon, 75
Jones, Thomas ap Catesby, 80
Jones, William, 40
Julia case, 95

Keane, John, 80
Kent Island (Va.), 56
Kentucky, 20, 28, 44, 51, 96
Kentucky rifle, 4, 23, 119
Key, Francis Scott, 77
King, Rufus, 120
Kingston (Ont.), 41, 46
Korean War, 1

Laffite, Jean, 79
Laffite, Pierre, 79
Lake Borgne, Battle of, 79–80
Lake Champlain, 50, 87; Battle of, 66–67
Lake Erie, 26, 29, 41–42, 49, 61, 65; Battle of, 43–44, 46, 58; U.S. vies for control of, 41–43
Lake Ontario, 41, 46–47, 49, 65–66
Lambert, Henry, 36
Lambert, John, 81
Lawrence, James, 57–58
Lawrence, USS, 43, 58

Lee, "Light-Horse" Harry, 98
Lee, Robert E., 98
Leipzig (Germany), 59–60, 95
Leopard, HMS, 8
Levant, HMS, 84
Lewiston (N.Y.), 49
Library of Congress, 74
licenses, British, 15, 93, 95
Lingan, James M., 98
Linnet, HMS, 66
Little Belt incident, 10
Liverpool (England), 84
Liverpool, Lord, 106, 109
Lloyd's (of London), 84
loans, U.S., 55, 88, 91–92, 99, 116–17
Lockyer, Nicholas, 80
Long Island Sound, 94
Louisiana, USS, 80
Louisiana Purchase, 100
Lowndes, William, 93
Lundy's Lane (Ont.), Battle of, 62–64, 103

Macdonough, Thomas, 3, 66–67, 86, 120
Macedonian, HMS, 36–37
Mackinac (Mich.), 27–29, 61, 67, 85, 109
Macomb, Alexander, 66–67, 86, 120
Macon, Nathaniel, 55
Madison, Dolley, 73
Madison, James, 5, 7, 21, 27, 86, 119; annual
    message of (1811), 12; and British attack on
    Washington, 72–74; and elections, 88–90;
    and Federalist opposition, 97, 116; and Henry
    affair, 12–13; and peace negotiations, 104–6,
    112; and restrictive system, 93, 95; and scare-
    crow party, 18; and success of war, 113; and
    war bill, 17; as war leader, 1, 88, 116; war mes-
    sage of, 15–16
Maine: British occupation of, 70, 83, 86; and
    peace negotiations, 107, 109–10
Malcolm's Mills (Ont.), Battle of, 61
manufacturing, 69
Marines, U.S., 47, 73–74
maritime issues: as cause of war, 2, 16–17, 19,
    104–6; U.S. failure to win concessions on,
    110, 112, 117
maritime war, 12, 16–17, 98. *See also* naval war;
    privateers
Marshall, John, 120
martial law, 82
Massachusetts, 70, 96–97, 99–102
Massias, Abraham, 77
Maumee River, 26, 28, 42

McArthur, Duncan, 61
McClure, George, 48–49
Melville Island (Halifax), 96, 119
merchantmen, arming of, 16–17
Mexican War, 1
Miami Indians, 28
Michigan Territory, 26
middle states, 95
militia, Canadian, 26. *See also individual battles
    and campaigns*
militia, U.S., 2, 12, 19–20, 37, 87, 96, 113, 120;
    casualties of, 117; condition of, 21; and
    conscription, 90; costly and inefficient, 91,
    116; and Jackson, 83; and New England,
    99–100, 118; refusal of to serve outside U.S.,
    26, 30, 44, 50, 65; refusal of to serve under
    Armstrong, 74; use of authorized, 12. *See also
    individual battles and campaigns*
Miller, James, 62–64
mines (underwater), 84
Minnesota, 107–8
Mississinewa, Battle of, 28
Mississippi River, 78, 80, 117; and peace nego-
    tiations, 107, 110
Mississippi Territory, 52
Mitchell, George B., 65
Mobile (Ala.), 57, 78–79
mob violence, 98, 116
money. *See* finance
Monroe, James, 74; and Battle of Bladensburg,
    73; favors maritime war, 16; impact of war on
    career of, 3, 120; jealous of rivals, 74, 88; and
    peace negotiations, 104–6, 112; and scarecrow
    strategy, 14
Monroe (Mich.). *See* Frenchtown (Mich.)
Monroe County (Ala.), 52
Monroe-Pinkney Treaty, 8–9, 14, 97, 104, 111
Montreal, 20, 66, 110; and U.S. campaign of
    1812, 31; and U.S. campaign of 1813, 48–50;
    and U.S. strategy, 23, 26, 40–41
Moose Island (Maine), 70
Moraviantown (Ont.), 44–45
Morrison, Joseph W., 50
"Mr. Madison's War," 1
Murray, John, 49
Myers, Ned, 46

Nantucket (Mass.), 69, 85
Napier, Charles, 56
Napoleon (Bonaparte), 74, 121; abdicates and
    exiled to Elba, 60; and Battle of Leipzig, 59,
    95; and Continental Decrees, 9; and Hun-

dred Days, 118; and retreat to France, 60; and Russian campaign of 1812, 38–39, 105
Napoleonic Wars, 5, 81, 115
national bank, 6–7, 92–93, 116, 120
national debt, U.S., 6, 91–92, 117
national honor, 2
National Intelligencer, Washington, 74
nationalism, 118
Nautilus, USS, 37
naval war: in campaign of 1812, 34–38; in campaign of 1813, 56–58; in campaign of 1814, 71, 83–84; on Lake Champlain, 66–67; on Lake Erie, 41–43; on Lake Ontario, 41, 46, 65; support for, 12, 16–17. *See also* privateers
Navy, Royal (British), 16, 33–34, 37, 87, 96; and blockade, 54–55, 68–69; and coastal raids, 55–56, 68–78; and conciliation, 14; and Gulf Coast campaign, 78–82; and impressment, 2, 8, 118; on the inland lakes, 41–42, 46, 65–57
Navy, U.S., 3, 37, 58, 89, 117; after 1800, 6, 12, 16, 23, 32–33, 90–91; after war, 119–20; and enemy merchantmen, 37, 84; Federalist support for, 6; manning of, 33, 90, 116; pay and bounties of, 33; in 1790s, 6, 99; and U.S. morale, 38, 120. *See also* naval war
navy yards: British, 33, 43, 47; U.S., 49, 74, 83
Nelson, Lord, 43
neutral rights, 6, 8–9, 12, 105–6, 110, 112
Newark (Ont.), 48–49
New Bedford (Mass.), 99
New Brunswick (Canada), 70
New England: and banks, 100; and British blockade, 54, 69; and British licenses, 95; and British raids, 69–70, 77; and conscription, 90; and defense costs, 99–100; economy of, 70, 95, 100; and elections, 90; and fisheries, 110; and Hartford Convention, 100–2; and Henry affair, 13; and separate peace, 112
New Orleans, 55; Battle of, 1, 3, 77–83, 86, 102–3, 118, 121; and peace negotiations, 109–10; and smuggling, 94–95
New York City, 23, 58, 65, 112
New York State, British invasion of, 49–50, 65–68
Niagara, USS, 43
Niagara Falls, 62
Niagara front: and campaign of 1812, 26, 29–30; and campaign of 1813, 40, 47–49; and campaign of 1814, 62–65
Nicholson, Joseph, 60
non-exportation act, 13, 93
non-importation act: of 1806, 9; of 1811, 15, 93–95

non-intercourse act, 9
Norfolk (Va.), 55–56
Norristown (Penn.), 98
North Point (Md.), Battle of, 76
Northwest. *See* Old Northwest
Norton, John, 30, 62
Nova Scotia, 70
nullification, 90, 101

"Old Hickory." *See* Jackson, Andrew
"Old Ironsides." See *Constitution*
Old Northwest, 3; and campaign of 1812, 26–29; and campaign of 1813, 42–46; and campaign of 1814, 61; and Indian war, 4, 10–11, 16, 46, 107
Old Republicans, 88
Old Southwest, 1, 4, 51–54, 118
Oneida Indians, 65
opposition to war. *See* Federalist party; Republican party
Orders in Council: adopted, 9; as cause for war, 2, 11–2, 15–17; and license trade, 15; and peace negotiations, 104, 110; repealed, 15
ordnance department, U.S., 22
Oswego (N.Y.), Battle of, 65
Oswego Falls (N.Y.), 65
Otis, Harrison Gray, 99, 101

Pakenham, Edward, 79–81
Paris (France), 59–60, 74
Paris, Treaty of (1783), 107, 110
Parker, Peter, 75
Patapsco River, 76–77
Patuxent River, 71–72
peace negotiations, 66, 78, 104, 107–11
Peace of Christmas Eve, 2, 107–13, 120
Peacock, HMS, 37, 57
Peacock, USS, 84
Pea Island (La.), 80
Pechell, Samuel J., 55
Pelican, HMS, 57
Penguin, HMS, 84
Pennsylvania, and elections of 1812, 89–90
Pennsylvania rifle, 4, 23, 119
Pensacola (Fla.), 51, 78–79
Perry, Oliver H., 3, 43–47, 54, 58, 120
Pettipaug (Conn.), 69
Phoebe, HMS, 83
Pig Point (Md.), 71, 73
Pike, Zebulon, 31, 40, 46–47
Plattsburgh (N.Y.), 31, 50; Battle of, 66–67, 86, 109
Plumer, William, 98

Point Peter (Ga.), 77

politics, 2, 87–88. *See also* Federalist party; Republican party

Popham, Stephen, 65

Porter, David, 83, 120

Porter, Peter B., 21, 64

Potawatomi Indians, 28

Potomac River, 73, 75, 98; Eastern Branch of, 72

powder, gun, 22, 34

Prairie du Chien (Wisc.), 61, 67, 85, 109

Preble, USS, 66

preparedness, military, 5–6, 12, 119–20

President, USS, 10, 32, 34, 83

Presque Isle (Penn.), 41, 43

prestige (national), 2

Prevost, George, 19, 61, 94; and armistice of 1812, 104; and Battle of Plattsburgh, 66–67; and Battle of Sackets Harbor, 49–50

Prince-de-Neufchatel, U.S. privateer, 85

Prince Regent, 74

prisoners of war: British, 96–97; French, 56; U.S., 42, 69, 96–97, 116, 118–19

privateers, British/Canadian, 37

privateers, French, 6

privateers, U.S., 7, 16–17, 69, 75, 87, 91; in campaign of 1812, 37; in campaign of 1813, 58–59; in campaign of 1814, 84–85, 107; and casualties, 117; and Federalists, 99; manning of, 33–34; and prisoners of war, 96, 119

Procter, Henry, 28, 42–45

Prophet, the, 10, 32, 117

Provincial Marine, British, 41

Put-in-Bay (Ohio), 43

quartermaster department, 22

Quasi-War, 6, 16, 33

Quebec (City), 20, 27; and British occupation of Maine, 70; and peace negotiations, 107, 109; and U.S. strategy, 23, 40

Queen Charlotte, HMS, 43

Queenston Heights (Ont.), Battle of, 29–31, 41, 97

Queenstown (Md), 56

Quincy, Josiah, 12–16, 120

Raisin River. *See* River Raisin

Randolph, John, 19–20

Rattlesnake, U.S. privateer, 59

Rattlesnake, USS, 84

recess, congressional, 14

Red Eagle, 51, 54, 117

Red Jacket, 62

Red Sticks, 51–54

Reed, Philip, 75

Reindeer, HMS, 84

"Remember the Raisin," 28, 45

Republican party: Broad objectives of, 5; and causes of war, 2, 17, 18; and declaration of war, 13–18; and factionalism, 11, 18, 88, 116; impact of war on future of, 120–21; and wartime elections, 88–90

restrictive system: futility of, 115; prewar, 9, 11, 14; wartime, 93–96

Rhode Island, 100–101

Riall, Phineas, 49, 62–63

rifles, 4, 23, 119

River Raisin, 26; massacre at, 28–29, 51–52

Robertson, James (Philadelphia Federalist), 112–13

Robertson, James (Royal Navy officer), 67

Rodgers, John, 34

Rodrigues Canal (La.), Battle of, 81

Ross, Robert, 72–74, 76

Rossie, U.S. privateer, 37

Russell, Jonathan, 104, 106

Russia, 38–39, 74, 105–6

Sackets Harbor (N.Y.), 41, 46–47, 50, 62, 65; Battle of, 49–50; and carrying of cable, 65–66

Salaberry, Charles de, 50

Santo Domingo, 79

Saranac River, 66

Saratoga (N.Y.), Battle of, 66

Saratoga, USS, 66–67

Savannah (Ga.), 55, 98

Savary, Jean B, 79

Sawyer, Herbert, 34

Scarecrow party, 12, 14, 18, 103

Scorpion, USS, 61

Scott, Hercules, 64

Scott, Winfield, 1, 3, 31, 40, 86, 120; on army officers, 21; and Battle of Fort George, 47–48; and Battle of Queenston Heights, 30; and Niagara campaign of 1814, 62–63

Scourge, U.S. privateer, 59

Scourge, USS, 46

Secord, Laura, 48

sectionalism, 118

sedition law, 6, 116, 118

Senate, U.S., approves peace treaty, 112. *See also* Congress, U.S.

Shannon, HMS, 47

Sheaffe, Roger, and Battle of York, 37

Sheffey, Daniel, 115

slaves: in Chesapeake, 55–56, 72; and Creeks, 51; and Gulf Coast campaign, 78; and Jack-

son, 118; and three-fifths clause, 102; and
　Treaty of Ghent, 111
Smith, Samuel, 75
Smyth, Alexander, 20, 29–30, 120
South, U.S., 7, 11, 17, 89, 92, 95
Southwest, 1, 4, 51–54, 118
Spain, 51, 59, 66, 72, 78, 94–95, 109. *See also*
　Florida; Navy, Royal (British), Gulf Coast
　campaign; Pensacola (Fla.)
Spanish-American War, 1
specie, 92, 100, 116
Springfield (Mass.), 22
Stamp Act Congress, 100
"Star-Spangled Banner, The," 1, 4, 77
State Department, U.S., 74
states' rights, 118
Stewart, Charles, 84, 120
St. Lawrence, HMS (schooner), 85
St. Lawrence, HMS (ship-of-the-line), 65
St. Lawrence front, 87; and British supply
　lines, 23; and campaign of 1812, 23, 26; and
　campaign of 1813, 50–51, 54; and campaign
　of 1814, 66
St. Lawrence River, 23, 50, 54
St. Marys River, 77, 94
St. Michaels (Md.), 56
Stoney Creek (Ont.), Battle of, 48, 72
Stonington (Conn.), Battle of, 69
St. Petersburg (Russia), 105
strategy, U.S, 16, 87; in 1812, 23–26, 31, 34; in
　1813, 40–41, 46–47; in 1814, 60–61
Stricker, John, 76
submarines, 84
Syren, USS, 84

Talladega (Ala.), Battle of, 52
Tallapossa River, 52
Tallushatchee, Battle of, 52
Tangier Island (Va.), 71
taxes: British, 109; U.S., 6–7, 9, 12, 55, 69,
　88–92, 116, 120
Taylor, Robert B., 56
Tecumseh, 10, 42–45, 51
Tenedos, HMS, 57
Tennessee: and Creek War, 52; and Gulf Coast
　campaign, 79–80
Tenskwatawa, 10, 32, 117
territorial expansion, 2, 19–20, 107, 118
territorial waters, U.S., 7
Thames, Battle of, 3, 44–46, 61, 103, 120
Thornton, William (British army officer), 80–81
Thornton, William (U.S. superintendent of
　patents), 74
"Those are regulars," 62

Ticonderoga, USS, 66–67
Tigress, USS, 61
Tingey, Thomas, 74
Tippecanoe (Ind.), Battle of, 11, 28
"To Anacreon in Heaven," 77
Tompkins, Daniel D, 3, 49
Toronto (Ont.). *See* York
torpedoes, 84
trade, U.S.: and British blockade, 54–55, 69–70;
　with enemy, 56, 69–70, 93–96, 116; and
　Madison's war message, 15–16; and restrictive
　system, 9; in 1790s, 6; threatened by Euro-
　pean belligerents, 2, 6–9
trade restrictions. *See* restrictive system
Trafalgar, Battle of, 34, 57, 67
Treasury Department, U.S., 55, 74, 92, 96, 116
Treasury notes, 92, 112
Treaty of Ghent, 2, 107–13, 120
Treaty of Paris (1783), 107, 110
Tripolitan War, 33
True-Blooded Yankee, U.S. privateer, 59
Twelfth Congress. *See* War Congress

"Uncle Sam," 32, 118
United States, USS, 32, 36
Upper Marlboro (Md.), 72
Urbana (Ohio), 26

Valparaiso (Chile), 83
Van Rensselaer, Solomon, 29–30
Van Rensselaer, Stephen, 29–30
veterans' benefits, U.S., 117
Vienna, Congress of, 106–9
Vietnam War, 1
Villeré, Jacques, 80
Villeré's Plantation (La.), Battle of, 80
Vincent, John, 47–48
Vineyard Sound, 94
Vixen, USS, 37
volunteers, U.S., 12, 19, 21, 87

War Congress, 11–18
War Department, U.S., 20–23, 31, 74
War Hawks, 11–15, 88, 91, 93
War of 1812: casualties of, 117; causes of, 12,
　17–18; costs of, 117; legacy of, 3–4, 117–21; ob-
　scurity of, 1–2; outcome of, 2, 86, 110, 112–13,
　115, 117; as second war of independence, 3,
　16–18, 113, 115
war preparations, 12–13
Warren, John Borlase, 54–56, 78
Washington (D.C.), 5; occupied by British, 1,
　72–74, 77, 83, 86, 103
Washington, George, 1, 5–6, 73–74

Washington, USS, 84

Wasp, USS (18 guns), 37

Wasp, USS (22 guns), 84

Waterloo (Belgium), Battle of, 118

Weatherford, William, 51, 54, 117

Webster, Daniel, 90, 120

Wellington, Duke of, 69, 79, 109–10, 121

West, U.S.: condition of militia of, 21, 23; and declaration of war, 17, 26; economic impact of war on, 85; and election of 1812, 89; and Hartford Convention, 102; and legacy of war, 117–18

West Indies: and Royal Navy, 33; and U.S. privateering, 58; and U.S. slaves, 72; and U.S. trade, 8, 54, 95, 105

White House, 73–74

Wilkinson, James, 50–51, 120

Willcocks, Joseph, 62

Winchester, James, 28

Winder, William, 48, 72–73

Wolfe, HMS, 46

Wool, John E., 30–31

Woolsey, Melancthon, 65

World War I, 1, 118

World War II, 1, 3

Wright, Robert, 18

Yankee, U.S. privateer, 37

Yeo, James, 41, 46, 65

York (Ont.), 41; Battle of, 46–47

DONALD R. HICKEY is a professor of history at Wayne State College in Wayne, Nebraska. He is the author of seven books, including *Don't Give Up the Ship! Myths of the War of 1812,* and numerous articles.

The University of Illinois Press
is a founding member of the
Association of American University Presses.

University of Illinois Press
1325 South Oak Street
Champaign, IL 61820-6903
www.press.uillinois.edu